Sounds, Syllable
Word Stress

Sounds, Syllables and Word Stress

Elementary and Intermediate English Pronunciation Practice

Dr Nsebeng Jean Mayala

To Jill Baker

With my best wishes

Dr Jean Mayala

First published in the UK in 2024 by Shakspeare Editorial

Copyright © 2024 Dr Nsebeng Jean Mayala.

ISBN 978-1-7392549-7-1 (paperback)
ISBN 978-1-7392549-8-8 (ebook)

Design www.ShakspeareEditorial.org

IN LOVING MEMORY OF

Mamono Mayungana Hélène
Katanga Kiongo Stanislas
Kangundu Nsil'afa Justin
Kangundu Kossy Justin (brother and friend)

You left fingerprints of love and devotion on our lives.
You shall not be forgotten.

CONTENTS

FIGURES

TABLES

TEXT BOXES

PHONEMIC SYMBOLS

Consonants

/b/	bank, number, tub	/d/	day, lady, head
/g/	girl, giggle, egg	/p/	pot, paper, cup
/t/	teach, hotel, boat	/k/	cat, cucumber, lack
/v/	vein, review, give	/ð/	this, father, bathe
/z/	zinc, present, was	/ʒ/	genre, measure, beige
/f/	fall, often, cliff	/θ/	thought, method, bath
/s/	say, passport, bless	/ʃ/	shell, bushman, dish
/h/	hot, behind	/ʧ/	cheese, achieve, clutch
/ʤ/	gender, algebra, courage	/m/	moon, memory, team
/n/	note, renew, ten	/ŋ/	ink, kingdom, morning
/w/	water, subway, wow	/j/	yes, beyond
/l/	lost, willing, tall	/r/	rain, forest, far away (link with following word)

Vowels

/iː/	be, leap, key	/ɪ/	hit, lip, ending
/e, ɛ/	bet, desk, care	/æ/	bag, sand, apple
/ɜː/	girl, first, circle	/ʌ/	but, drum, brother
/uː/	crew, food, fruit	/ʊ/	book, could, full
/ɔː/	call, baseball, thought	/ɒ/	motto, octopus, upon
/ɑː/	car, hard, park	/ə/	(schwa) about, bitter, calculator

PREFACE AND ACKNOWLEDGEMENTS

My first debt of gratitude goes to the British Council who kindly sponsored my four-year study at Durham University. Your financial assistance and a great deal of other material support made it possible for me to successfully achieve the objective set by your department. I am grateful for being one of the recipients of your scholarships.

Secondly, I would like to sincerely thank Peter Grundy, professor at Durham University, who not only introduced me to research skills, but was also my guide and mentor for four years. Peter spent a great deal of time and effort to support and help me successfully complete my PhD degree.

I am immensely grateful to Pete Gentry for his in-depth proofreading and expert editing suggestions to improve the book content and presentation. Pete's attention to details – style, font, and consistency – helped turn a draft of ideas into structured and meaningful content.

My sincere thanks to Angie A. Phillips for expertly drawing the many brilliant and colourful diagrams used in this book. Such illustrations are likely to prove particularly useful for beginner and younger learners.

And finally, I would like to express my wholehearted appreciation to Alison Shakspeare for her time, effort and dedication in seeing this book to publication. My sincere thanks for turning my wish into a reality.

WORDS OF GRATITUDE TO
FAMILY AND FRIENDS

It is hoped that this book will inspire a noticeably young generation of children to always give the best of themselves while hopefully becoming true advocates of the book. As it is not possible to include all the young children from our large family, I only mention here those who are fortunate to share memories of our everyday lives: grandchildren Jacob Kimanese Moseley, Samuel Makangu Kiwanuka-Musoke, Jaden Kossi Moseley and Sophia Ngahel Kiwanuka-Musoke; niece Taliah Kala; grandniece Naomi Pandanzyla and nephew Michael Bwelesi. Those young grandchildren, nieces and nephews not mentioned here are equally loved and always part of our family life.

I would like my children and their spouses, namely, Linda and Jason, Christian, Jean-Junior, Hélène and Paul, and my wife Jeannette Kimpiabi Mayala to see this book as a gift to you for being part of my everyday life. Similarly, I am grateful to my sister Micheline Makibengi, her children and grandchildren, younger brothers Justin Kangundu, Paulin Bwelesi as well as my in-laws Annie and Joseph Kimpiabi for sharing part of your lives with my young family in its early and challenging years.

A big thank you to all my friends and their families for playing a special role in my life, namely, Herman Rapier, Raphael Kamidi, Idesbald Munganga, Annie Nzinga, Sister Rosemary, Sister Margaret, Christine Makala, Bernard Munganga, Dominique Mputubwele, Makele Ben-And, Anatole Nzwanga, Scholastique Kingalala, André Biselela, Venant Munungi, Rigobert Lufalanka, Kitila Mkumbo, Deogratius Wenga, Agnès Mondo, Bruno Matudi, Christina Nantwi, Antoinette Tshabola and many others not included here for always keeping alive our common memories.

I am also deeply thankful to all my colleagues and friends at the Virtual School in Barking and Dagenham: Jane Hargreaves, Ian Starling, Jill Baker, Lynne Hannigan, Janet Cassford, Angelina Ikeako, Rukhsana Bakhsh, Cris Ford, Kathleen Twin, Fahmeeda Ghulam, Kathleen Adams, Tricia Butler, Hannah Anderson and Efrem Berhane, for your friendship and support throughout our shared professional lives. My work in schools was made interesting and rewarding thanks to special friends like Tracey Whittington and colleagues such as Gary Anderson and Emma Somers.

Special thanks to my daughters Linda and Hélène, to Phillippe Kodi, Fahmeeda Ghulam and Stephanie Bwelesi for your encouragement and constant reminders to complete the book.

Also, my warm and heartfelt thanks to all my students at the Institut Pédagogique National in Kinshasa and to all my tutors and students at Kinampanda Teachers' College (Tanzania) for your contribution to several practical aspects in this book.

Last but not least, I would like to express my love and sincere appreciation to all my extended family members and family friends: the Kangundus, the Bwelesis, the Makangus, the Tamulombos, the Kahungus, the Kimpiabis, the Pandanzylas, the Moseleys, the Kiwanuka-Musokes, the Kodis, the Kukwikilas, the Agobas, the Kalas, the Ghulams, the Grecus, the Mapanda-Meyas, the Kwilus, the Mukasa Mukengis, the Munungis, the Bulabulas, the Bakas, the Kaulus, the Kindembis, the Mukezas, the Sally-Lutus, the Sukidisas, the Makukas, the Kihanukas, the Kisendes, the Totos, the Bundukis, the Witeles, the Zengamambus and many others not included for your continued love and friendship and for sharing so many good memories together.

INTRODUCTION

1. WHY THIS BOOK?

The academic and social pressure on all teacher trainees to master the English language in a French-speaking environment could only be overcome by a strong and unparalleled motivation to succeed. To be able to complete three academic years of undergraduate studies and two years of graduate studies in the English department at the Institut Pédagogique National in Kinshasa, we had to be highly motivated and extremely hard-working students.

With our starting point being almost no English, we had to work hard for two long years as undergraduate students before we began to relax and enjoy English lessons. The main motivating factor was the arrival in the English department of a British teacher, Mr Alan Barr.

The weekly listening lessons delivered by Mr Barr in the language laboratory were a source of truly funny and animated conversations. All the fuss was caused by the sight of our twisting and twisted mouths trying hard to correctly articulate the English sounds. There was a need for (and a huge interest in) all of us to learn to speak well so that we could impress our lecturers and the other French-taught students at the college. To give the reader an idea of how much we enjoyed practising our new language, try to exaggerate the pronunciation of the following sentence while watching your mouth in a mirror:

> *The wrong man was arrested by the security forces.*

You will be surprised to see the variation in the movements of the mouth, particularly the lips and the tongue. This is what we used to do to impress the other students who were not taking English. Although we were all being trained to become teachers, some of us had a higher ambition: to go to England and get a university degree in teaching English. When we were offered the job of assistant lecturers in the English department, we felt we had taken the first giant step towards achieving our ambition. Two years into the job, after taking a series of written and oral tests and having successfully passed them, we were given the unexpected opportunity to study in England for the first time.

On arrival in London, we were accommodated at a hotel on Gloucester Road. The next day, when we asked the receptionist for directions to the nearest shops, we got our first shock of the English accent. Whatever the receptionist said, none of us registered a single word. At that point, we realised how far behind our level of understanding of spoken English was. We were glad our students were not around at that very embarrassing moment. That first difficult conversation set the tone for the rest of our one-year stay in the United Kingdom (UK).

It is this personal experience, first as students and later as lecturers, that contributed partially to the idea of writing a book. Another motivating factor came about during the time we worked as advisory teachers in the London Borough of Barking and Dagenham, supporting pupils who spoke English as an additional language. The influx of secondary school children from abroad, with little or no English on arrival in the UK, prompted our service to become more proactive in finding a variety of strategies to support these children. As teachers, we were required to have a better understanding of some of the basic features of pronunciation and how they interact in improving spoken language.

Our third and perhaps most powerful motivation to write this book came from our two-year stay in Kinampanda, at a teachers' training college in the north of Tanzania. We were hired by the British Council as ELT (English language teaching) trainers to help college tutors improve their English teaching methodology. The job included collaborative English lesson planning with college tutors, observing English lessons and providing feedback to tutors, and producing appropriate resources for teachers in secondary schools. Advice and help were offered to address potential methodology challenges. Despite their varying levels of English knowledge, the students' and tutors' commitment and continued interest to deliver good English language lessons gave us additional reason and motivation to urgently complete this book.

2. WHO IS THIS BOOK FOR?

The three major groups of readers described in Section 1, that is, college students training to teach English, college tutors of English and lecturers in English departments, will all benefit from the content of this book. In fact, knowing how to speak a language does not necessarily imply being able to teach it or even less so being able to describe the different aspects of that language.

Native speakers use the language unconsciously; they do not need to know – and certainly do not care – what linguists say or write about the words or sentences they use. However, it is important that students preparing to teach English, including native speakers, are introduced to some basic phonological terminologies such as *consonants, vowels, syllables, word stress*, ones that constitute the starting point when learning pronunciation.

This book is therefore aimed at the English language students and teachers who need to explore these essential terminologies when focusing on the spoken form of the English language. The book offers descriptions and examples of concepts at the elementary and intermediate levels.

The examples in Tables I.1–I.4, taken from the book, illustrate those levels of pronunciation practice.

Table I.1. Elementary level – describing the sounds of English

Vowel	Examples
/i:/	be, leap, key
/ɜ:/	girl, first, circle
/ʌ/	but, drum, brother

Consonant	Examples
/ð/	this, father, bathe
/θ/	thought, method, bath
/tʃ/	cheese, achieve, clutch

Table I.2. Pre-intermediate level – describing syllable division and marking stress

One-syllable words	Two-syllable words	Three-syllable words
book	about	calendar
bus	bookcase	computer
come	famous	library
road	picture	manicure
short	traffic	popular

Pre-intermediate students will include those who have some prior understanding of pronunciation concepts such as consonants, vowels and the articulation of sounds generally. They may therefore be introduced to topics such as syllables and stress marking.

Table I.3. Intermediate level – connected speech

Example	Pronunciation	Connected speech
Good morning	/gʊd mɔ:nɪŋ/	/gʊ mɔ:nɪŋ/
How do you do?	/haʊ dʊ jə du:/	/haʊdjədu/
Would you like tea or coffee?	/wʊd ju laɪk ti: ɔ: kɒfɪ/	/wədʒu laɪk tiə kɒfi/
Could I have some sugar, please?	/kʊd ai hæv sʌm ʃʊgə pli:z/	/kʊdai həv səm ʃʊgə pli:z/

At the intermediate level, students have a good understanding of basic conversational English. They can use common phrases such as greetings and can ask basic questions with some degree of accuracy. They have a good range of vocabulary and can use it appropriately. They may not speak English with the required fluency and still need more practice to achieve this.

Table I.4. Upper-intermediate level – basic conversational English

Example	Conversation in connected speech*
A: Good morning. How can I help you, sir?	|| gʊd ˈmɔ:nɪŋ haʊ kənaɪ hɛlp jʊ sə||
B: Good morning. We would like to go for a holiday in Zanzibar.	|| gʊd ˈmɔ:nɪŋ widˈlaɪk təgəʊ fə hɒlɪdeɪ ɪn ˈzænzɪbɑ: ||
A: When would you like to go?	|| wɛn wʊdʒu laɪk tə gəʊ ||
B: Possibly in November 2020	|| pɒsɪbli ɪn nəʊˈvɛmbə twɛnti twɛnti ||

* The transcriptions of connected speech are purely for illustration. We do not claim they are completely accurate nor do we say that they are the only way natural speech sounds can be represented.

Students at the upper-intermediate level can express themselves intelligibly with some degree of fluency. They have a good understanding of intermediate-level concepts, and, more importantly, students may work independently using available resources. However, if they want to progress to an advanced level, the students may need to attend formal teaching in a college or university.

3. How is the book organised?

The book is divided into seven sections. Each of the first six sections describes a given concept, providing as much theoretical detail as necessary to help with the understanding of the idea from a linguistic point of view. Each section ends with a set of practical activities related to the concept described in the section. The seventh section is mainly practical, offering examples of connected speech. Also, all transcriptions are based on the General British English models.

The practical activities at the end of each section offer students the opportunity to revisit their understanding of the concepts described. An important feature of these activities is that they are devised as research questions. This means students must revisit the section to search for answers unless they have prior knowledge of the topics. It is only through careful reading of the material in the section that students will be able to find answers to the activities. However, for those who cannot find the appropriate answers, these are provided at the end of the book for each activity. This theory–practice approach is used to stimulate focused reading as well as discussions among students, while offering them relative freedom in the way they answer the questions.

A brief description of each section follows, with its specific focus.

A. Description and classification of speech sounds

The focus in this section is on articulatory phonetics, that is, on the production of speech sounds. We provide a detailed description of articulatory phonetics and briefly outline acoustic phonetics (the study of sound movement through the air) and auditory phonetics (the study of sound perception). From the *where* (bilabial, dental, palatal and so on) and the *how* (stop, fricative, nasal and so on) to the distinction between *voiced* and *unvoiced*, the production of speech sounds covers a whole range of patterns. Our focus is on the description of articulators (tongue, palate, teeth and lips) and the roles they play in the production of sounds. The description is intended to provide students with a better understanding of *where* and *how* sounds are articulated.

Although the production of vowels appears straightforward, students – particularly second-language learners – may need more practice to be able to determine where in the mouth (front/high or low/back) the specific vowel sounds are produced.

B. Introducing some basic concepts

In Section B, we define the concept of a sound as a phoneme. A phoneme is the smallest sound unit that can convey meaning. In the minimal pair cat /kæt/ and bat /bæt/, the sounds /k/ and /b/ are two different phonemes because they differentiate the meanings in a similar context: /æt/. Phonemes are therefore sound units that carry meanings.

A vowel sound can occur either on its own or with another vowel. When two vowels occur together in the same syllable, they form a diphthong. There are eight diphthongs in English. Here are three examples: *face* /eɪ/, *five* /aɪ/ and *now* /aʊ/.

Similarly, consonants can occur either alone or in sequences of two or three. When they occur in sequence, they form a cluster. A consonant cluster is a blend of consonants without a vowel between them. The following are examples of clusters: *brain, flat, splash* and *strong.*

There are special consonant combinations that create completely new sounds: these are known as digraphs. For example, the letter <c> combined with the letter <h> is pronounced /ʧ/, as in the words *chalk* and *church.*

C. English sounds and their spellings

Section C demonstrates that there is an imbalance between the number of letters (26) used to spell words and their corresponding sounds in English (44). Such an imbalance means that students may not know how to *say* some of the letters in words or sentences. Several sound representations – of certain letters – may be completely different from their spelling forms.

The difference between letters and sounds also means that a given letter or combination of letters may be pronounced differently when it occurs in different positions within a word. Also, when some letters combine with other letters, this may produce entirely different sounds; for example, <c> with <h> produces a different sound: /tʃ/.

The consonant /r/ plays an important role in the English sound system. When used in certain contexts, such as after a vowel, the /r/ sound can trigger a change in the vowel sound, as in the words *girl* or *first*. However, in final position, the <r> is either silent (not pronounced) or it may trigger a change of the vowel sound, turning it into a schwa /ə/, as in the words *bitter* and *calculator*. Silent letters are present in the written form of the word but are not pronounced.

D. Stress within root words

This section uses everyday vocabulary to introduce students to the concept of a syllable. When students master the idea of one syllable, they can easily tackle two-, three- or multiple-syllable words. In this way, students will gradually improve their understanding of the principles behind the syllable concept as well as those of marking the stress on complex words. The difference between words and syllables is:

Word	Vowel letters	Vowel sounds	Syllables
cat	one vowel letter (a)	one vowel sound /æ/	one syllable
come	two vowel letters (o, e)	one vowel sound /ʌ/	one syllable
nature	three vowel letters (a, u, e)	two vowel sounds /ei/ /ə/	two syllables

When a word has two or more syllables, it must be marked with *stress* to determine its meaning. The *stressed syllable* is pronounced *louder*, *higher* and *longer* than the unstressed syllables. The difference between **per**mit (noun) and per**mit** (verb) is made clear by the position of the stress within these two words – here marked in bold letters. Similarly, the number of syllables is determined by the number of vowel sounds one hears, not by the number of letters in the word, as illustrated by the word *nature*.

E. Stress within complex words

Words with affixes can be clearly described according to their structures: there are distinct differences between inflectional and derivational affixes. All inflectional affixes are suffixes, that is, they are added at the end of the root words, such as plural forms and regular past tenses. Inflectional affixes only affect the grammatical structure of the word; they do not change the meaning of the word, nor do they affect the position of the stress. Unlike inflectional affixes, derivational affixes can be added either at the beginning (as prefixes) or at the end (as suffixes) of the root word. While all derivational affixes affect the meaning of the root word, not all of them will trigger a shift of the stress.

Some inflectional affixes may add an extra syllable to the root word, and, more importantly, the pronunciation of the added syllable may be affected in certain contexts. A typical example of this phenomenon can be seen in the case of the regular past tense <ed> being pronounced /t/ in *asked*, /d/ in *enjoyed* and /ɪd/ in *waited*. Derivational affixes can add one or more syllables to the root word in addition to changing the meaning of the word. When a derivational prefix is added to the root word, it generally carries the primary stress, as in *rail – derail*; *possible – impossible*; *behave – misbehave*. However, when a derivational suffix is added, there may be two possibilities:

a) the derivational suffix does not affect the position of the stress, as in *correct – correction*; *race – racism*; *piano – pianist*

b) the derivational suffix triggers a shift of the stress to a different position, as in *define – definition*; *possible – possibility*; *courage – courageous*.

Another type of complex word described in Section E is a *compound word*. A compound word is a combination of two or more words that means one thing. The words in a compound word can occur independently elsewhere. There are three types of compound words: closed compounds, open compounds and hyphenated compounds, as in the examples *bookmark*, *car ferry* and *well-being* respectively. Stress placement in closed compound words follows a similar pattern as in single words. Open compound words are treated as separate single words. There is still a lot of debate on whether hyphenated compound words should be treated as separate or single words. Whereas stress placement in the first two categories (closed and open) follows existing patterns, the last category (hyphenated) continues to be problematic.

F. Aspects of connected speech

Section F outlines the way native speakers of English use longer structures like phrases and sentences. Phrases and sentences constitute the starting point of spoken language. When two or more words are spoken together, speakers link the pronunciation of the sounds between the words to produce smooth and continuous speech. Some of the main features of connected speech include contraction, elision, consonant-sound linking, vowel-sound linking, strong and weak syllables, tonic stress and contrastive stress.

Connected speech is strongly characterised by the distinction between stressed (strong) and unstressed (weak) syllables. The use of unstressed sounds makes English particularly difficult for second-language students, mainly because the unstressed sounds, often realised as schwa, are less audible and less distinguishable. In the sentence *Peter is going to the shop to buy some eggs,* all the underlined words are pronounced quickly and are therefore less audible to the listener.

The word that carries the 'tonic stress' in a sentence is the most important word for the speaker. In neutral speech, native speakers usually emphasise words which are towards the end of the sentence. However, the speaker can decide to shift the stress to the word they want to carry their main message. Second-language students should be encouraged to pay particular attention to the speaker's focus on what they want to express.

G. Effective communication in English

In the last section of the book, we highlight the importance of using the correct standard pronunciation, not only when learning English but also when expressing yourself in English. Using intelligible speech is essential in communicating effectively in spoken language. Correct pronunciation implies the correct use of stress, knowing the linking strategies and using the right intonation.

Placing the stress in the wrong position within words such as *record* or *project* may give the listener a different message to the one intended. Similarly, a speaker of English who stresses every single syllable will not only sound odd but completely fail to effectively communicate their intended message. The use of weak forms, as contrasted with strong forms, will make the speech sound smooth and melodic. In particular, the schwa sound /ə/, found in most weak forms, is one of the main features that characterises the English spoken language.

The rest of the section offers examples of phrases, sentences and short conversations to illustrate the use of connected speech. It concludes by affirming that all transcriptions used in the book are based on General British English. However, as already highlighted in Table I.4, the transcriptions of connected speech in this book are purely for illustration. We do not claim they are completely accurate nor do we say they are the only way natural speech sounds can be represented.

A. DESCRIPTION AND CLASSIFICATION OF SPEECH SOUNDS

The first section of the book focuses on the articulation of speech sounds, offering a description of the way sounds are produced. Such a detailed description of the articulation of individual speech sounds is also known as 'articulatory phonetics'. In addition to articulatory phonetics, we also briefly describe the other two related aspects of phonetics: acoustic phonetics, which studies sound movement through the air, and auditory phonetics, which deals with the way speech sounds are perceived by the listener.

Through articulatory phonetics, it is possible to pinpoint where in the mouth certain sounds are produced, such as *bilabial consonants* /p/, /b/ and /m/ – their production involves both lips – or to tell whether consonants are *voiced* or *unvoiced* by feeling whether the vocal folds *vibrate* during the production of those consonants. The production of vowels, however, requires a little bit more practice to be able to determine where in the mouth (front/high or low/back) the specific vowel sounds are produced.

A1. THE PHYSIOLOGY OF SOUND PRODUCTION

There are three branches of phonetics that deal with the physiology of sound production and perception: articulatory phonetics, acoustic phonetics and auditory phonetics.

Articulatory phonetics

This is the branch of phonetics that deals with the actual production of speech sounds. In other words, articulatory phonetics deals with where and how sounds are produced in the mouth. In Section A2, we provide a more detailed description of sound production together with a diagram of all the organs involved in the production of speech sounds.

Let us take an example to illustrate articulatory phonetics. To pronounce the initial sound of the word *book*, we put our two lips together to stop the flow of air from the lungs, then we release it. The subsequent sound produced, /b/, is called a bilabial stop, from the Latin word *labia* (meaning lips) and *bi* (meaning two).

However, to produce the initial sound of the word *this*, we bring the tip of the tongue against the upper teeth and force the air through the narrow passage to make the sound /ð/. A detailed analysis of these processes is given in Section A2.

Acoustic phonetics

When people are engaged in a conversation, the expectation is that there is at least a speaker and a listener. The sounds produced by the speaker – in words, sentences or songs – travel through the air to reach the listener. Acoustic phonetics studies the physical properties of sounds during their journey from the speaker's mouth to the listener's ear. A full description of the physical features of sounds requires special equipment and scientific knowledge. One needs good knowledge and understanding of sound waves, amplitude, frequency and pitch. We have taken a deliberate position not to provide a detailed description of acoustic phonetics because, in the context and purpose of this book, such a specialised account is not necessary. However, we offer here some essential concepts to help students have some understanding of what we mean by acoustic phonetics. These basic concepts include vibration, sound waves and frequency.

Vibration occurs when a sound hits the air. Different sounds produce different sorts of vibration: rapid vibrations have high frequency while slow vibrations have low frequency.

A sound wave can be defined as a sound travelling through a succession of vibrations. The faster the vibrations the emitted sound makes, the higher the pitch. Figure A.1 offers a visual representation of a sound wave.

The frequency of a sound wave refers to the number of times the waveform completes one full cycle within a second.

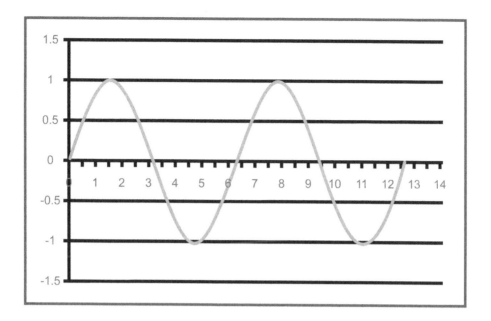

Figure A.1. A visual representation of a sound wave – time (in milliseconds)

The x-axis (horizontal line) represents the period of time it takes a sound wave to complete a cycle, usually calculated in seconds or milliseconds. The y-axis (vertical line) represents the amplitude of the sound wave or the height of the wave; this is calculated in decibels. © N. Jean Mayala

Auditory phonetics

While articulatory phonetics deals with the production of sounds, auditory phonetics focuses on the perception of sounds, that is, how we hear sounds and interpret them. If the speaker (articulating sounds) is the initiator of verbal communication, the listener is the recipient (hearing and interpreting sounds), with acoustic phonetics in the middle.

The main sensory organ responsible for sound reception is the ear. This is divided into the outer ear, the middle ear and the inner ear. We briefly describe here the path followed by sound from the outer ear to the brain.

Step 1: The outer ear

The outer part of the ear (also known as the pinna) collects the sound energy and increases the sound pressure that enters the ear canal until it reaches the eardrum (or tympanic membrane). This is a very fine membrane that separates the ear canal and the middle ear.

Step 2: The middle ear

When the sound hits the eardrum, it makes the membrane vibrate. The vibration transforms the sound wave into mechanical vibration patterns which then enter the inner ear.

Step 3: The inner ear

The inner ear consists of three small bones: the malleus, the incus and the stapes. Having gone through the three bones, the mechanical vibrations are sent to the cochlea, the major sensory organ of the inner ear, whose function is to transform (through a complex system) mechanical vibrations into electrical signals that can then travel to the brain.

It is worth noting that the inner ear also contains special receptor cells which help with both locating the origin of the sound and maintaining equilibrium. Figure A.2 shows the anatomy of the ear.

A cross-sectional view of the human ear

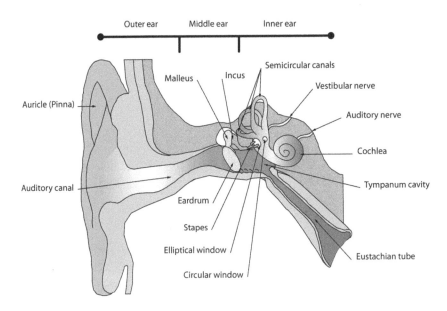

Figure A.2. A cross-sectional view of the human ear
© N. Jean Mayala

A2. THE SPEECH ORGANS

The process through which human beings produce sounds is known as 'articulation'. Unlike other animals, human beings are born with the ability to produce speech sounds. However, the production of sounds for speech requires the person to learn how to use their main speech organs appropriately. Those speech organs can be organised into three main groups: the lungs, the larynx (including the vocal folds/cords) and the vocal tract.

The lungs

The lungs play the role of 'power supply', providing airflow to the larynx. They are the main source of energy for our vocal activities. Although in most human languages people use the airflow from the lungs to speak, in some languages, people also use other sources of energy to produce sounds like clicks and implosives.

The larynx and the vocal cords

The larynx contains a series of cartilages, muscles and ligaments, among which are the vocal folds or vocal cords. The vocal folds are defined as two small bands of elastic tissue stretching between the front and the back of the larynx. When we produce speech sounds, the vocal cords take one of these three different positions:

a) They can be wide apart, allowing the air to flow freely.
b) They can be firmly pressed together, thus blocking the airflow from the lungs.
c) They can be moving, opening and closing very quickly.

O'Connor (2013) explains that during the production of 'voiced' sounds such as /b/, /m/ or /v/, or the production of vowel sounds like /iː/ or /e/, the vocal folds open and close very quickly – around 800 times a second. This rapid process is perceived by the ear as *voice*. The technical term used to describe *voice* in articulation is *vibration*.

The vocal tract

The vocal tract consists of the nasal cavity (the passage through the nose) and the oral cavity (the passage through the mouth). All the articulators are found in the vocal tract. These include the palate (soft, hard and alveolar ridge), the tongue (tip, front, blade and back), the teeth (upper and lower) and the lips. The main function of these articulators is to modify the sound waves into recognisable units known as speech sounds. All the articulators described are illustrated in Figure A.3.

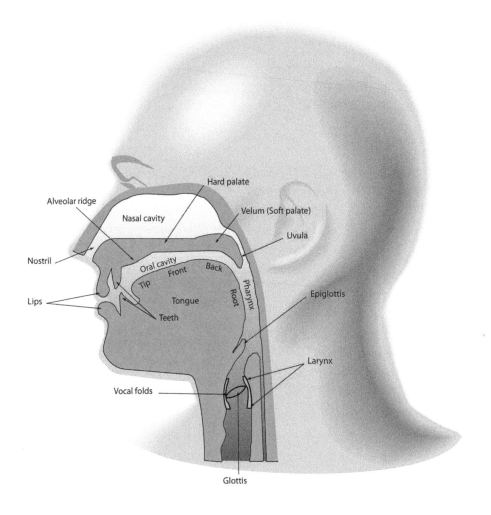

Figure A.3. The main organs used in the production of speech sounds
© N. Jean Mayala

A3. THE ARTICULATION OF CONSONANT SOUNDS

To produce sounds, the human body uses an airstream from the lungs. In the production of consonant sounds, this airstream is either blocked or partially restricted at some point in the vocal tract. If, during production, the vocal folds open and close rapidly, the air flowing past them will cause the folds to vibrate (move). The sounds produced with the vocal folds vibrating are known as *voiced* sounds, and those sounds produced without vibration are known as *voiceless* or *unvoiced*.

Different parts of the mouth are used in different positions to produce specific sounds – this is the place of articulation. Similarly, some sounds are produced with different types of constriction or turbulence or with different amounts of force – this is the manner of articulation. Both place and manner of articulation are described in detail in the next section.

At the end of each set of sounds, a text box provides students with a list of concrete examples of words starting with those sounds combined with different vowels, to illustrate the level of frequency and complexity of sound use in English.

Place of articulation of consonants

Place of articulation refers to *where* in the mouth the articulation of the sound takes place. The aim of learning about articulation is twofold:

1) To give students the opportunity to identify the differences between sounds in the way they are produced in the mouth.

2) To provide a visual representation of the sounds through their transcription (transcription is a written record of the sound as it is said, as transcribed in dictionaries).

There are 24 consonant sounds in English. They are described below according to where they are produced in the mouth.

Bilabial

The bilabial sounds /p/, /b/ and /m/ are produced by bringing both lips (the labia) together. However, in the production of /m/, the air escapes through the nose. The bilabial /w/ involves a narrowing of the vocal folds and a rounding of both lips.

Labiodental

The lower lip is pressed against the upper front teeth to produce the sounds /f/ and /v/.

(Inter)dental

The tip of the tongue is placed against the upper teeth for the sounds /θ/ and /ð/.

Alveolar

The tip of the tongue touches the alveolar ridge (the part of the mouth just behind the upper teeth). The following sounds are all produced at this position: /t/, /d/, /s/, /z/, /n/ and /l/. The air escapes (a) through the nose during the production of /n/, and (b) from both sides of the tongue when producing the sound /l/.

Palato-alveolar

The sounds in this group are produced with the blade of the tongue (the blade is the part immediately behind the tip) creating a narrow opening with the beginning of the palate (the roof of the mouth). The sounds produced at this position include /ʃ/, /ʒ/, /tʃ/ and /dʒ/.

Palatal

The only palatal sound, /j/, is produced by bringing the middle of the tongue close to the hard palate.

Velar

The back of the tongue touches the velum (the soft palate); the sounds /k/, /g/ and /ŋ/ are articulated at this position. For /ŋ/, the air escapes through the nose.

Glottal

The sound /h/ is produced in the glottis. The glottis is the opening between the vocal folds in the throat.

Manner of articulation of consonants

The correct articulation of a consonant sound depends on two key elements: first, its position in the word, and second, on the sound that follows. In the context and purpose of this book, we will discuss and illustrate the articulation of consonant sounds in *initial position* followed by a vowel. Adding vowel sounds to the articulation of consonants provides further evidence that vowel letters are not always pronounced in the same way, even when they are used in similar position, such as in the examples *duck*, *duty* and *duvet*.

Similarly, the same consonant can be followed by all five vowel letters, <a>, <e>, <i>, <o> and <u>, as in *paper, pen, pipe, police* and *pupil*. However, in a few cases, certain consonants are only followed by a limited number of vowel letters. The consonant <g> pronounced /ʒ/, as in *genre* and *gendarme*, is one example.

Stops (also known as plosives)

During the production of the six plosives – two bilabial sounds, /p/ and /b/, two alveolar sounds, /t/ and /d/, and two velar sounds, /k/ and /g/ – the airflow is stopped before being released in a small explosion. Figures A.4–A.6 illustrate the articulation of stop sounds.

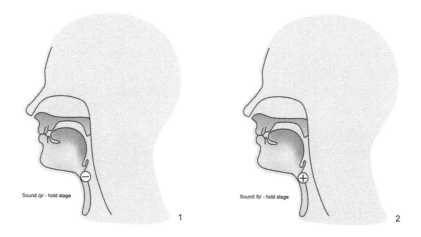

Figure A.4. Articulation of the bilabial stop sounds /p/ and /b/

The consonant sounds /p/ and /b/ are commonly known as stops or plosives. The airflow from the lungs is stopped at the lips. After the stricture, the air is then released. The two articulators that come together in the production of /p/ and /b/ are both lips (the labia). The sounds are produced by bringing together the lips and are therefore called bilabial stop sounds. The first bilabial stop sound, /p/, is produced without the vibration of the vocal folds (unvoiced), whereas the second bilabial stop sound, /b/, involves the vocal folds vibrating (voiced).

The feature 'unvoiced' is represented on the diagrams by a minus sign (–) at the throat level, whereas the 'voiced' feature is represented by a plus sign (+).

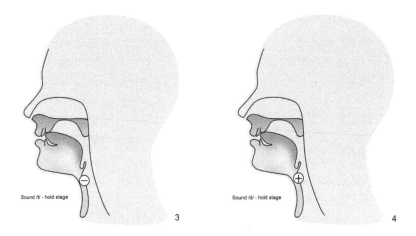

Figure A.5. Articulation of the alveolar stop sounds /t/ and /d/

The sounds /t/ and /d/ are called alveolar stop sounds. During the articulation of the alveolar sounds, the airflow is stopped by the tip of the tongue moving against the alveolar ridge (this is the part of the mouth just behind the upper teeth). Then the air is released with plosion.

Like bilabials, alveolar stops are produced in pairs – the /t/ stop sound is unvoiced and the other sound, /d/, is voiced.

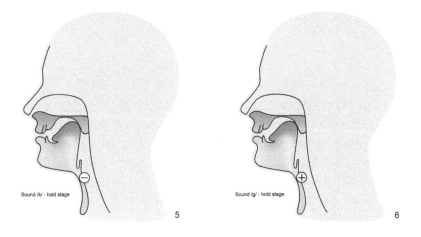

Figure A.6. Articulation of the velar stop sounds /k/ and /g/

The sounds /k/ and /g/ are known as velar stop sounds. The airflow from the lungs is blocked temporarily by the back of the tongue pressing against the velum (the soft palate), then it is released with a small explosion. The voicing is caused by the vibration of the vocal folds. Thus, the sound /k/ is unvoiced, whereas the sound /g/ is voiced.

Text box A.1. Words beginning with stop sounds

/b/	baby	beach	big	boat	buffet
	ball	beauty	bike	body	bug
	bar	bed	bitter	bouquet	bully
/p/	paper	peace	piece	poetry	public
	park	peer	pipe	police	pump
	parent	pen	pitch	pool	pupil
/d/	daddy	dear	diary	doctor	duck
	dark	deaf	dinner	dog	duty
	dance	deck	dirty	door	duvet
/t/	table	teacher	tidy	toast	tuition
	tall	teenage	tin	tongue	tummy
	task	text	time	tower	turn
/g/	game	gear	gift	goal	guard
	garden	get	girl	goggle	guilty
	gather	gecko	give	good	guru
/k/	kale	kebab	kind	kola	kudos
	karate	keep	king	Koran	Kurdish
	karaoke	keynote	kitchen	korma	kuru
/k/	café	celt	-	cold	cub
	cake	ceilidh	-	colour	curly
	call	Celtic	-	come	cute
/k/	character	chela	chianti	cholera	-
<ch>	chalcedony	chelonian	chimera	choleric	-
	chalybeate	chemistry	chiropody	cholesterol	-

Fricatives

Fricatives constitute the largest number of consonant sounds in English, with a total of nine sounds. Unlike stops, fricatives are produced by restricting the airflow at different points in the vocal tract and forcing the air through the constriction. One fricative, the glottal sound /h/, is produced by forcing the air through the narrow passage between the vocal folds.

The other eight fricatives are described here in pairs. Four of them, /v/, /ð/, /z/ and /ʒ/, are voiced (vocal folds vibrating) and the other four, /f/, /θ/, /s/ and /ʃ/, plus the glottal /h/, are unvoiced (no vibration of the vocal folds).

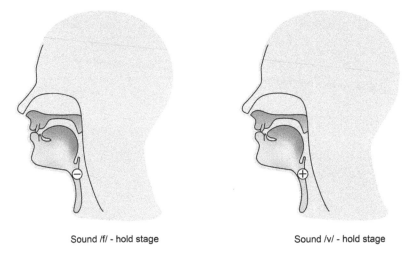

Sound /f/ - hold stage   Sound /v/ - hold stage

Figure A.7. Articulation of the labiodental fricative sounds /f/ and /v/

To articulate the labiodental sounds /f/ and /v/, the airflow is forced through a narrow gap between the lower lip and the upper front teeth. The /f/ sound is unvoiced while /v/ is voiced.

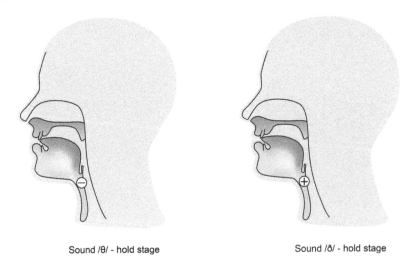

Sound /θ/ - hold stage   Sound /ð/ - hold stage

Figure A.8. Articulation of the dental fricative sounds /θ/ and /ð/

To articulate the dental sounds /θ/ and /ð/, the tip of the tongue approaches the upper teeth, leaving a narrow passage between them through which the airflow forces its way.

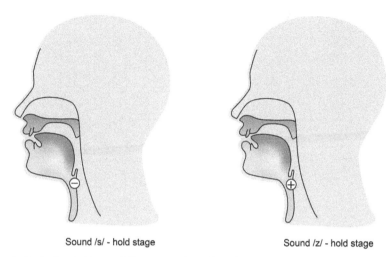

Sound /s/ - hold stage   Sound /z/ - hold stage

Figure A.9. Articulation of the alveolar fricative sounds /s/ and /z/

In the articulation of the alveolar sounds /s/ and /z/, the tip of the tongue gets very close to the alveolar ridge, forcing the air between the two.

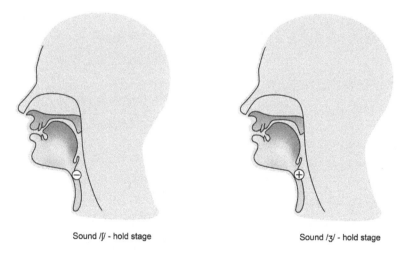

Sound /ʃ/ - hold stage   Sound /ʒ/ - hold stage

Figure A.10. Articulation of the palato-alveolar fricative sounds /ʃ/ and /ʒ/

The palato-alveolar fricative sounds /ʃ/ and /ʒ/ are articulated by constricting the airflow through a narrow opening between the blade of the tongue and the palate (the roof of the mouth).

Text box A.2. Words beginning with fricative sounds

/f/	face	fear	fiction	fog	full
	factor	ferry	fight	food	fun
	fall	fever	first	fork	fuse
/f/	phase	pheasant	philately	phonetics	phut
<ph>	phalange	phenelzine	philology	phonology	-
	pharmacy	phenol	philosopher	phosphate	-
/v/	vacant	vehicle	victory	voice	vulture
	valley	veto	violent	volley	vulnerable
	vast	verdict	virtue	voucher	vulpine
/z/	zany	zeal	zigzag	zombie	zucchini
	zarf	zebra	zinc	zone	Zuni
	zareba	zero	zip	zoo	Zulu
/s/	sad	sea	sick	society	subject
	safe	second	side	some	suit
	salt	secret	sieve	soon	surge
/ʒ/	genre	gendarme	garage	-	-
/ʃ/	shadow	she	shift	shop	shuffle
	share	shell	shine	shoot	shut
	sharp	sheet	shirt	short	shufty
/ð/	that	the	this	those	thus
	than	their	thine	thou	-
	-	then	thither	though	-
/θ/	thanks	theme	thing	thorn	thumb
	thaw	thesis	third	thunder	-
	thatch	therapy	thief	thousand	Thursday

Affricates

Affricates combine two sounds: a stop and a fricative. The production of an affricate starts like a stop but completes as a fricative. There are only two affricate sounds in English: /tʃ/ and /dʒ/. The sound /tʃ/ is unvoiced, while /dʒ/ is voiced.

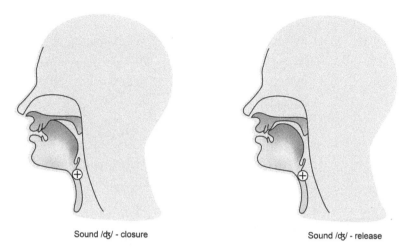

Sound /ʤ/ - closure   Sound /ʤ/ - release

Figure A.11. Articulation of the palato-alveolar affricate sound /ʤ/

The sound /ʤ/ is a voiced affricate. It is a blend of two sounds: the stop sound /d/ and the fricative sound /ʒ/. The airflow from the lungs is temporarily blocked by the tip and blade of the tongue pressed against the rear part of the alveolar ridge. At the same time, the front of the tongue is raised towards the hard palate, with the sides of the tongue touching the upper teeth. The air is then released slowly in the form of friction.

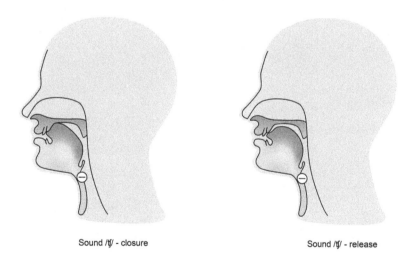

Sound /ʧ/ - closure   Sound /ʧ/ - release

Figure A.12. Articulation of the palato-alveolar affricate sound /ʧ/

The sound /ʧ/ is also an affricate, but it is unvoiced. The articulation process of /ʧ/ is similar to /ʤ/, described above. However, /ʧ/ starts as a /t/ sound and completes as a /ʃ/ sound.

Text box A.3. Words beginning with affricate sounds

/dʒ/ <j>	jacket	jealous	jibe	job	jubilee
	jade	jeep	jigsaw	jockey	judge
	jam	jerk	jingle	jogger	juice
/dʒ/ <g>	-	generous	giant	-	-
	-	genius	ginger	-	-
	-	gentle	giraffe	-	-
/tʃ/	chair	cheap	chicken	chocolate	chunk
	champion	cheeky	child	choice	church
	chapter	check	chilli	choke	churn

Nasals

The nasal sounds /m/, /n/ and /ŋ/ are all produced by stopping the airflow in the mouth but releasing it through the nose. Nasals are all voiced sounds.

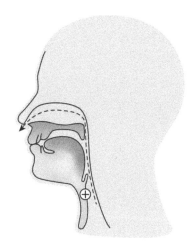

Figure A.13. Articulation of the bilabial nasal sound /m/

The nasal /m/ is a bilabial sound. To articulate /m/, the airflow is stopped by both lips pressed together, then the soft palate lowers to allow the air to exit through the nose (indicated by the arrow).

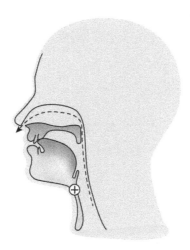

Figure A.14. Articulation of the alveolar nasal sound /n/

The nasal /n/ is an alveolar sound. The airflow is blocked by the tip of the tongue coming against the alveolar ridge, forcing the air to escape through the nose (indicated by the arrow).

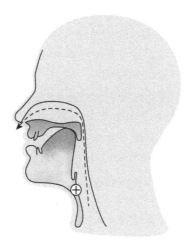

Figure A.15. Articulation of the velar nasal sound /ŋ/

The nasal /ŋ/ is a velar sound. To produce /ŋ/, the back of the tongue moves up and is pressed against the soft palate (the velum), allowing the air to exit through the nose (indicated by the arrow).

Text box A.4. Words beginning with nasal sounds

/m/	madam	meal	milk	mobile	mug
	make	measure	mind	money	music
	market	messy	mirth	mood	murky
/n/	name	neat	nice	noise	number
	natural	never	nickname	noon	numerous
	naughty	nerve	niece	now	nurse

Nasal /ŋ/ in medial position

	banknote	fishmonger	finger	handkerchief
	kangaroo	kingdom	language	nightingale
	penguin	younger		

Nasal /ŋ/ in final position

| | amazing | boxing | eating | king |
| | railing | plunk | song | young |

Approximants

There are a total of four approximant sounds: /w/, /j/, /l/ and /r/.

The sound /w/ is a rounded labio-velar approximant. The lips are rounded while the back of the tongue is raised towards the soft palate, making a narrow passage for the airstream.

The /j/ sound is a palatal approximant. During its production, the vocal folds are in a neutral position. The lips may be neutral or spread, usually ready to take the shape of the following vowel, as in *yes* or *yam*.

The lateral sound /l/ is produced by constricting the airflow through the sides of the tongue with the tip of the tongue against the alveolar ridge. This is the only lateral sound in English.

The typical English /r/ sound is described as a palato-alveolar approximant. To articulate the sound, the tip of the tongue is raised near to, but not touching, the rear of the upper part of the alveolar ridge. The middle part of the tongue is lowered, allowing the airstream to pass through without any friction. In some English accents, the tongue may be curled back slightly (retroflex), but in others, the /r/ may be trilled or rolled.

Text box A.5. Words beginning with approximant sounds

/w/	waiter	weald	wicket	woman	wurst
	wave	well	wild	work	wuthering
	water	west	willing	wonderful	wuss
/j/	yank	year	yield	yoke	yuck
	yard	yellow	yippee	young	Yule
	yawn	yes	yips	youth	yummy
/l/	lady	legal	liberty	lodger	lucky
	lamb	lemon	light	long	luminous
	large	ley	lieutenant	lonely	lurch
/r/	razor	receipt	rice	road	rubella
	rapid	registrar	rich	royal	rugby
	raw	reign	rimu	rose	ruse

Table A.1. Places and manners of articulation of English consonants

Place of articulation

Manner of articulation		Bilabial	Labiodental	Dental	Alveolar	Palato-alveolar	Palatal	Velar	Glottal	Labio-velar
Stops (plosives)	Voiced	b			d			g		
	Voiceless	p			t			k		
Fricatives	Voiced		v	ð	z	ʒ				
	Voiceless		f	θ	s	ʃ			h	
Affricates	Voiced					dʒ				
	Voiceless					tʃ				
Nasals	Voiced	m			n			ŋ		
Approximants	Voiced				l	(palato-alveolar) r	j			w

A4. THE ARTICULATION OF VOWEL SOUNDS

As demonstrated in Section A3, it is generally possible to determine the exact place of articulation of consonant sounds in the mouth, but it can take some practice to be able to locate where in the mouth vowel sounds are produced.

There are, however, some broad positions in the mouth where given vowel sounds are articulated: at the front of the mouth for front vowels, in the middle of the mouth for central vowels and at the back of the mouth for back vowels. Let us note that all vowel sounds are voiced. Their production always involves the vibration of the vocal folds, as described in Section A2. Here are the main English vowels with examples:

Text box A.6. Positions of articulation of vowel sounds

Front vowels	
/iː/	be, these, leap, key, see
/ɪ/	hit, lip, ending, himself, accident, ambition
/e/	bet, desk, assess, better, attention, phonetic
/æ/	bag, sand, apple, blanket, adjective, calendar
Central vowels	
/əː/	girl, first, circle, confirm, determine, turbulence
/ʌ/	but, drum, culture, brother, punctuation, supplement
/ə/	about, bitter, grammar, persuade, calculator
Back vowels	
/uː/	crew, food, fruit, two, shoe
/ʊ/	book, could, full, childhood, football, bulletin
/ɔː/	call, baseball, hallway, instalment
/ɒ/	motto, octopus, upon, salt
/ɑː/	car, park, garden, father

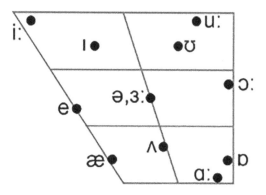

Figure A.16. Places of articulation of English vowels
© N. Jean Mayala

The distinction between vowels and consonants can be considered at three levels: physiological (at the articulation level), acoustic (at the level of sonority) and phonological (their function in the formation of syllables).

Physiological distinction

From an articulatory point of view, vowel sounds are produced with a free flow of the airstream. In contrast, during the production of consonant sounds, the airflow is either partially or fully constricted (blocked) somewhere in the oral tract.

Acoustic distinction

Vowel sounds are generally more sonorous (prominent) than consonant sounds. In the words *bet*, *cat* and *but*, the vowels *e*, *a* and *u* are louder than the consonants that surround them.

Phonological distinction

At the phonological level, a vowel sound constitutes the *nucleus* or centre of a syllable. Generally speaking, there is no syllable without a vowel sound. The role of consonant sounds in identifying syllables is peripheral. In a syllable, a single vowel may or may not be surrounded by consonants to form a syllable. In Section D, we offer a detailed description of the structure of a syllable as being composed of either a single vowel (V), as in *a*, a consonant plus a vowel (CV), as in *go*, a vowel and a consonant (VC), as in *egg*, or a consonant, a vowel and a consonant (CVC), as in *pen*.

A5. CLASSIFICATION OF SPEECH SOUNDS

Text box A.7. Classification of speech sounds

A. CONSONANTS

Place of articulation

Bilabial sounds	/p/, /b/, /m/
Labiodental sounds	/f/, /v/
(Inter)dental sounds	/θ/, /ð/
Alveolar sounds	/t/, /d/, /s/, /z/, /n/, /l/
Alveolar palatal sounds	/ʃ/, /ʒ/, /tʃ/, /dʒ/
Palatal sound	/j/
Palato-alveolar	/r/
Velar sounds	/k/, /g/, /ŋ/
Labio-velar	/w/
Glottal sound	/h/

Manner of articulation

Stop (plosive) sounds	/p/, /b/, /t/, /d/, /k/, /g/
Fricatives	/v/, /ð/, /z/, /ʒ/, /f/, /θ/, /s/, /ʃ/, /h/
Affricate sounds	/tʃ/, /dʒ/
Nasal sounds	/m/, /n/, /ŋ/
Approximants	/w/, /r/, /l/, /j/

B. VOWELS

Front vowels	/iː/
	/ɪ/
	/e/
	/æ/
Central vowels	/ɜː/
	/ʌ/
	/ə/
Back vowels	/uː/
	/ʊ/
	/ɔː/
	/ɒ/
	/ɑː/

SECTION A ACTIVITIES

ACTIVITY A1. HUMAN ORGANS OF SPEECH

Name the different parts of the human body that are used to produce speech sounds.

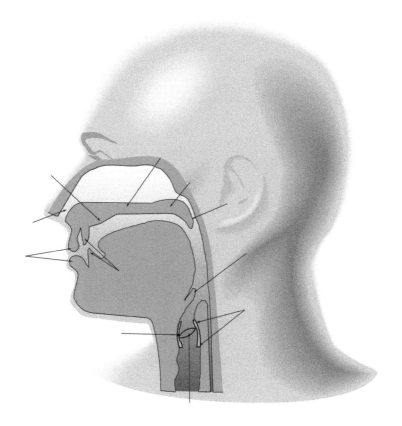

ACTIVITY A2. DESCRIBING SPEECH SOUNDS

What are these sounds called?

/b/, /p/, /d/, /t/, /g/, /k/

_____

Describe how these pairs of sounds are articulated.

/b/ and /p/

_____

/d/ and /t/

_____

/g/ and /k/

_____

ACTIVITY A3. MATCHING SOUNDS AND ARTICULATION

Match the sound with the way it is articulated (see the glottal example).

Sound	Symbol	Way it is articulated
Labiodental	/ʒ/, /ʃ/	The airflow goes through between the lower lip and the upper front teeth, close but not touching
Dental	/z/, /s/	The airflow goes through a narrow passage between the tip of the tongue and the upper teeth
Alveolar	/h/	The tip of the tongue gets very close to the alveolar ridge, forcing the air between the two
Palato-alveolar	/v/, /f/	The airflow is constricted through a narrow opening between the blade of the tongue and the palate
Glottal	/ð/, /θ/	The airflow is forced between the vocal folds

ACTIVITY A4. AFFRICATE SOUNDS

Read the following words; they all start with an affricate. Decide which words start with the sound /ʤ/ and which ones start with /ʧ/. Write them in the appropriate row. An example of each sound has been given.

child	jealous	cheap	ginger
cheeky	choice	giant	job

sound /ʤ/
generous

_____ _____ _____ _____

sound /ʧ/
cheese

_____ _____ _____ _____

ACTIVITY A5. APPROXIMANT SOUNDS

Highlight all the words with approximant consonants in initial position.

paper	lion	shoes	door	waiter
mother	simple	road	year	girl
jam	long	walk	lazy	razor
yell	van	red	yes	welcome

Now put all the highlighted words in their appropriate groups – one example has been given.

i) /l/   lion

_____ _____ _____ _____

ii)

_____ _____ _____ _____

iii)

_____ _____ _____ _____

iv)

_____ _____ _____ _____

ACTIVITY A6. COMPLETE THE MISSING SOUNDS

This is a table of the English consonants. There are <u>eight</u> consonant sounds missing, they have been replaced with a dash: _

Complete the eight missing consonants.

Place of articulation

Manner of articulation		Bilabial	Labiodental	Dental	Alveolar	Palato-alveolar	Palatal	Velar	Glottal	Labio-velar
Stops (plosives)	Voiced	b			d			_		
	Voiceless	_			t			k		
Fricatives	Voiced		v	ð	z	_				
	Voiceless		f	_	s	ʃ			h	
Affricates	Voiced					dʒ				
	Voiceless					_				
Nasals	Voiced	m			n			_		
Approximants	Voiced				l	(palato-alveolar) _	j			_

B. INTRODUCING SOME BASIC CONCEPTS

In this section, we define pronunciation as an important tool for effective communication. Unlike written language, spoken language requires suprasegmental features, such as stress and intonation, to make meanings clear. Pronunciation therefore refers to both the articulation of individual sounds (the segmental level) and the way sounds are used to convey meaning (the suprasegmental level). The suprasegmental level includes features such as stress, rhythm and intonation. English native speakers naturally use these features to make speech effective and intelligible to the listener.

At the centre of the segmental level, we have phonemes. A phoneme is the smallest sound unit that can convey meaning. In the minimal pair *cat* /kæt/ and *bat* /bæt/, the sounds /k/ and /b/ are two different phonemes because they differentiate the meanings in a similar context: /æt/. Phonemes are therefore sound units that carry meanings. Phonemes include both vowels and consonants.

A vowel sound can occur either on its own or with another vowel. When two vowels occur together, they form a diphthong, as in these examples: *face* /eɪ/, *five* /aɪ/ and *now* /aʊ/.

Similarly, consonants can occur either alone or in sequences of two or three. When they occur in sequence, they form clusters. A consonant cluster is a blend of consonants without a vowel between them, such as in the words *brain* and *flat*. All these concepts are described in detail in this section.

B1. THE DEFINITION OF PRONUNCIATION

It is generally accepted that pronunciation deals with both the production and the interpretation of speech sounds, with the ultimate purpose of conveying meanings. While articulation – see Section A – is specifically concerned with the production of individual sounds, pronunciation has a broader scope, including the understanding and interpretation of sounds in words and utterances. Pronunciation therefore refers to both (a) the production of individual sounds – the segmental level – and (b) how sounds are used to convey meaning – the suprasegmental level.

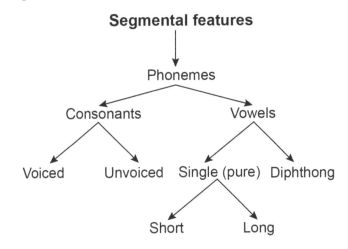

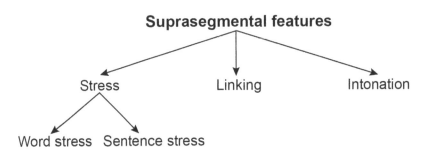

Figure B.1. Key features of English pronunciation

Segmental features are made up of the smallest units of the sound system of a language – here, English. At the lower end of pronunciation, students should be introduced to the production of individual sounds; this helps them to adapt their vocal tract to produce these new sounds. It is also an opportunity for students to hear and practise the differences between sounds. Those individual sounds, or *phonemes*, constitute the basic *units* or *segments* of a language. Thus, teaching students how to make the individual sounds of English constitutes the first step towards producing real speech.

Suprasegmental features are additional units of speech. They include stress, linking, intonation and body language. These features have the most effect on the quality of meaning or the intelligibility of the message. So, from sounds, students need to learn how to combine these sounds into words, how to mark the stress and how to control their intonation. For example, using the wrong stress or inappropriate intonation may affect the meaning or even convey a different meaning. Only a limited number of suprasegmental features are discussed in this book: they include sound linking and sentence stress. The suprasegmental features are summarised in Figure B.1.

B2. PHONEMES AND MINIMAL PAIRS

What is a phoneme? A simple answer to this question would be that any of the sounds we described in Section A (vowels and consonants) are phonemes. We know that the consonant sounds /b/ and /p/ are different phonemes because *bin* and *pin* are different words.

A phoneme is therefore the smallest sound unit which can convey a distinct meaning. According to Crystal (2003), when we refer to the English sound system, we are actually referring to the number of phonemes that are used in English and how they are organised. As further described below, we are talking not only about the differences between consonants but also the differences between consonants and vowels, between pure vowels and diphthongs and between voiced and unvoiced sounds. A list of English phonemes is given in Appendices 1 and 2.

On the other hand, a minimal pair/set is a group of words which are differentiated by one phoneme. The context '_ig' will produce different meanings or words every time a different consonant is placed in this position. Each consonant that makes the meaning of the context different is a phoneme. Thus, /b/, /p/, /d/ and /w/ are different phonemes because *big*, *pig*, *dig* and *wig* are different words.

Similarly, the context 'f_t' can be filled with different vowel sounds (phonemes) to produce different words. Words such as *fit*, *fat*, *foot* and *fought* have different middle vowel sounds; they are therefore different words.

There are other phonological features which are used to differentiate meanings between groups or pairs of words. We will describe three of them here.

Long vowel–short vowel contrast

The vowel sounds in these pairs of words are pronounced differently:
the first one is long, the second short. The difference in the length of
the two vowel sounds is the main feature that makes the meanings
of the words different.

Table B.1. Long–short vowel contrast

Long	Short
bean	bin
cord	cod
fool	full
sheep	ship
seat	sit

The position of stress

There are several words in English which are also known as word-
class pairs. These pairs of words with identical spelling differ from
each other by the different position of the stress. As a general
tendency, nouns and adjectives have their stress on the first syllable
while the equivalent verbs generally have their stress on the second
syllable. In the examples in Table B.2, the syllable with stress is
indicated in bold letters. A more detailed description of word-class
pairs is given in Section D.

Table B.2. Position of stress in noun–verb contrast

Noun	Verb
desert	de**sert**
export	ex**port**
object	ob**ject**
permit	per**mit**
record	re**cord**

Voiced–unvoiced contrast

The use of voiced and unvoiced sounds in similar contexts is
another feature that can distinguish meanings between two words.
The pairs of words in the following examples are different because
they have a voiced–unvoiced contrast in their initial sounds.

Table B.3. Voiced–unvoiced contrast of initial consonant sounds

Voiced	Unvoiced
veal	feel
zeal	seal
big	pig
dry	try
glue	clue

The first two pairs of words, /viːl/–/fiːl/ and /ziːl/–/siːl/, both have the same sound context: /iːl/. The difference in meanings between these words is the result of the voiced–unvoiced distinction of their initial sounds. To understand the practical differences between voiced and unvoiced sounds, try saying the following sounds without interruption with your fingers on your throat: start with /f/ immediately followed by /v/, then try the /s/ sound followed by /z/:

/ffffffffffffffffffffffffffffffffffffffffffvvvvvvvvvvvvvvvvvvvvvvvvvvvvvvvvv/

/ssssssssssssssssssssssssszzzzzzzzzzzzzzzzzzzzzzzzzzzzzzzz/

The first two sounds, /f/ and /v/, are articulated at the same position in the mouth, and the difference between them is that /f/ is produced without vibration of the vocal folds while /v/ involves the vocal folds vibrating. A similar explanation applies to the other two sounds, /s/ and /z/.

B3. HOMOPHONES

There are many words in English which are pronounced in the same way but spelt in completely different ways. They are called homophones. The difference between homophones is usually specified through their use in specific contexts, as shown in these examples:

The council members *meet* once a month.

We bought some *meat* at the abattoir.

Here are a few more examples of homophones:

Table B.4. Examples of homophones

dear	deer
peace	piece
sea	see
there	their
wait	weight
weak	week

B4. VOWEL SEQUENCES: DIPHTHONGS

Vowel sounds can occur alone or together with other vowels. When two vowels occur together in the same syllable, they form a diphthong. There are eight diphthongs in English, and they are represented in writing by a variety of spellings, as shown in Table B.5:

Table B.5. Vowel sequences: diphthongs

Diphthong	Examples			
/eɪ/	break	face	day	they
/ɔɪ/	boy	coin	noise	voice
/aɪ/	height	five	lie	my
/ʊə/	cure	poor	tour	sure
/eə/	care	chair	their	wear
/əʊ/	boat	know	old	sew
/aʊ/	down	house	now	town
/ɪə/	beer	fierce	here	near

Figure B.2 illustrates the articulation of diphthongs. The pronunciation starts from the first vowel sound then glides into the second vowel sound. A diphthong is therefore pronounced as one unit with two parts.

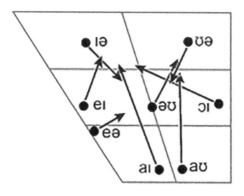

Figure B.2. Direction of diphthong articulation
© N. Jean Mayala

B5. CONSONANT SEQUENCES: CLUSTERS

Like vowels, consonants can occur in sequences of two, three or even four. A consonant cluster, or a consonant blend, can be described as a sequence of two or more consonants with no vowel between them. Note that there are very few four-consonant clusters, and they occur only in word-final positions. We will start with two-consonant clusters.

Two-consonant clusters

Many two-consonant clusters occur in familiar words and are therefore relatively easy to pronounce. Two-consonant clusters can occur in initial, medial or final position in words. There is a very large number of English words with two-consonant clusters in initial position, with some being rather specific to the English language.

Table B.6. Main consonant clusters in initial position

2nd / 1st	/l/	/k/	/r/	/m/	/n/	/p/	/t/	/w/
/b/	✓		✓					
/k/	✓		✓					
/d/			✓					
/f/	✓		✓					
/g/	✓		✓					
/p/	✓		✓					
/s/	✓	✓		✓	✓	✓	✓	✓
/t/			✓					✓

Table B.7. Two-consonant clusters in initial position

Cluster	Examples	Cluster	Examples
/bl/	blank, bless, blind, blood	/sk/	scary, scooter, score, scout
/br/	brain, brave, break, bright		skeleton, skirt, skull, sky
/dr/	drama, drill, drive, drug	/sl/	slaughter, slave, slide, sleep
/fl/	flat, floor, flower, fluent	/sm/	small, smell, smoke, smooth
/fr/	fraction, free, frozen, fruit	/sn/	snake, sneak, sneeze, snow
/gl/	glance, glory, globe, glue	/sp/	space, spend, spoon, sports
/gr/	grammar, green, grocery, group	/st/	station, stereo, stomach, study
/kl/	clan, clean, click, clock	/sw/	swan, sweet, switch, swim
/kr/	crane, creative, crown, cruel	/tr/	train, tree, tripod, trust
/pl/	play, please, plot, plural	/tw/	twenty, twice, twin, twist
/pr/	practice, pretty, primary, problem		

Three-consonant clusters

Compared with two-consonant clusters, the number of three-consonant clusters in initial position is rather limited, except where the first consonant of the cluster is <s>. There are more three-consonant clusters in final position. Nearly all three-consonant clusters in initial position start with /s/ followed by a stop sound. The examples in Table B.8 offer an overview of possible initial-cluster sequences:

Table B.8. Three-consonant clusters in initial position

Cluster	Examples
/skr/	scratch, screen, scream, script
/skj/	skewer (/skjʊə/)
/skw/	square, squash, squeeze, squirrel
/spl/	splash, split, splint, splendid
/spr/	spray, spread, spring, sprint
/stj/	stupid (/stjuːpɪd/)
/str/	straight, street, stress, strong

In final position, there are more three-consonant clusters, especially when we include plural forms and regular past tenses. This also explains, in part, why in normal speech, one of the consonants is either reduced or simply dropped in these clusters.

Let us consider a few examples.

Table B.9. Three-consonant clusters in final position

Cluster	Examples	Spoken form
	lists	/lisːs/
/sts/	costs	/kɒsːs/
	tests	/tesːs/
/sks/	masks	/masːs/
	desks	/desːs/

Regular past tense with <ed>

The case of three-consonant clusters with regular past tense in final position requires further explanation. The -ed ending in the words in Table B.10 is pronounced without sounding the <e>. The <d> is pronounced /d/ if the sound before <e> is voiced, as in the example *arranged*, where the /ʒ/ sound is voiced. The <d> is pronounced /t/ where the <e> follows an unvoiced sound, as in the example *helped*, where /p/ is unvoiced. The omission of <e> can be challenging for some groups of students whose tendency will be to put an /ə/ or an /e/ vowel between the consonants, producing words such as /əreɪnʒəd/ instead of /əreɪnʒd/.

Table B.10. Three-consonant clusters with regular past tense

Cluster	Examples
/ldʒd/	bulged, indulged
/ltʃt/	belched, filched
/lkt/	bulked, milked, sulked
/lpt/	helped, scalped, pulped
/lvd/	involved, resolved, solved
/mpt/	jumped, limped, stamped
/mft/	triumphed
/nʃt/	drenched, launched, pinched
/nʒd/	arranged, changed, sponged

B6. Special clusters: digraphs

One of the key features that distinguishes English from many other languages is the mismatch between letters and their sounds, described in detail in Section C. This is particularly evident in vowels. It should be emphasised that while most consonants and consonant clusters are pronounced as they are spelt, there are special combinations of consonants that create completely new sounds: these are called *digraphs*. The most common digraphs in English are illustrated in Table B.11:

Table B.11. Special consonant clusters: digraphs

Possible letter combinations	New sound created
c + h	/tʃ/
s + h	/ʃ/
p + h	/f/
t + h	/θ/ or /ð/
w + h	/w/

Text box B.1. Digraphs in different positions within words

Digraphs at the beginning of words

ch	=	/ʧ/	chair, chalk, church
sh	=	/ʃ/	shake, shine, shoe
th	=	/θ/	thin, thick, thousand
th	=	/ð/	this, then, there
wh	=	/w/	why, when, where
ph	=	/f/	pharmacy, phoneme, photograph

Digraphs in the middle of words

ch	=	/ʧ/	enchanting, exchange
ph	=	/f/	morphology, philosophical
sh	=	/ʃ/	Englishman, washing
th	=	/θ/	authority, mathematics
th	=	/ð/	northern, without

Digraphs at the end of words

th	=	/θ/	bath, moth
ng	=	/ŋ/	king, ring
ck	=	/k/	chick, duck
sh	=	/ʃ/	fish, wash
ch	=	/ʧ/	church, ditch

Digraph sounds are particularly challenging for learners who speak phonetic languages. The tendency will be for students to add a vowel between the consonants or to simply pronounce the consonants as they are spelt. Some typical examples often heard include replacing the sounds /ð/ or /θ/ with /t/ for words like *this* and *thin*.

SECTION B ACTIVITIES

ACTIVITY B1. SIMILAR SOUNDS BUT DIFFERENT SPELLINGS

What do you call words which sound the same but are spelt differently, such as *week* and *weak*?

_____

Give three examples of such words:

_____

_____

_____

ACTIVITY B2. SOUND VOICING

Hold your throat with your hand and say the following words, focusing on their initial sounds: *face*, *safe*, *shop*, followed by *voice*, *zoo*, *genre*. Repeat the activity twice. You should feel some *vibration* inside the throat when you say three of the initial sounds.

What do you call those sounds which are produced with vibration?

_____

List the words:

_____

_____

_____

And what do we call the other sounds produced without vibration?

_____

_____

List the words:

_____

_____

ACTIVITY B3. REGULAR PAST TENSE WITH <ED>

The regular past tense <ed> forms used in the following sentences are pronounced differently. Practise reading aloud each sentence. Underline/highlight the regular verb (as in the example) and decide in which category you would include the verb.

1) The court <u>rejected</u> his not-guilty plea.
2) As a child, I believed the earth was flat.
3) My mum helped me finish my homework.
4) Jacob and Samuel enjoyed playing in the park.
5) Life in the village reminded me of my childhood.
6) The police officer asked to see her driving licence.

Now write down the verbs on the lines below, next to the correct endings – the first one has been done for you.

/ɪd/   rejected

_____   _____

/d/

_____   _____

/t/

_____   _____

ACTIVITY B4. CONSONANT SOUND SEQUENCES

Here are five consonant sounds: /b/, /d/, /k/, /l/, /r/. Combine them in as many ways as possible to create meaningful new words, as illustrated in the example.

/b/ + /r/	as in	**brain**	**bread**
	as in		
	as in		
	as in		
	as in		

ACTIVITY B5. SPECIAL SOUND COMBINATIONS

Some sound combinations can produce completely new sounds. Give two examples of words with the new sounds.

c + h   →   /tʃ/

_____   _____

p + h   →   /f/

_____   _____

t + h   →   /θ/

_____   _____

t + h   →   /ð/

_____   _____

s + h   →   /ʃ/

_____   _____

C. ENGLISH SOUNDS AND
THEIR SPELLINGS

O'Connor (2013) in *Better English Pronunciation* reminds us that 'written English and spoken English are obviously very different things' (p. 1). He goes on to observe that 'letters and sounds must never be mixed up. Letters are written, sounds are spoken' (p. 7). Therefore, knowing letters cannot help us pronounce words we do not know. It follows from this view that students learning English will not know for certain how given letters are pronounced without having learnt their corresponding sounds. In phonetic languages like Lingala and Kikongo, however, where a given letter represents a given sound, the speaker knows how to pronounce the letter as that letter is also the sound.

English uses only 26 letters – from the Roman alphabet – to produce thousands of words. In spoken English, however, those 26 letters are represented by 44 individual sounds or phonemes. These 44 phonemes can be combined in thousands of different ways to produce an unlimited range of words that compose the English language. There are even more sound combinations when one includes the different dialects and accents of English.

One, therefore, has to be careful not to confuse letters and sounds. But it is also important to note that most of the English consonant sounds – 17 out of 24 – are pronounced as they are spelt. Understanding the difference between letters and sounds also implies that the speaker is aware that the number of sounds in a word *is not always equal* to the number of letters needed to write it.

One of the ways one can differentiate between letters and sounds (in English) is to consider how the different letters are represented as sounds. Vowels, more than consonants, have a larger variation of sound representations. The vowel letter <a>, for instance, is represented by a far larger number of different sounds than the consonant letter <c>, which only has a limited number of sounds, as described later in the section.

C1. VOWEL LETTERS AND THEIR SOUNDS

The five vowel letters are responsible for the production of hundreds of sounds in English.

We will start with the first vowel <a>, which happens to be the first letter of the alphabet. There are six main sounds represented by the letter <a>: /æ/, /ɑː/, /ɔː/, /ə/, /ɒ/ and the diphthong /eɪ/. From our experience of working with second-language students, the first three sounds are less challenging than the fourth, /ə/. One of the reasons is that the schwa sound /ə/ is softer and has a lower pitch. Also, the sound is not expected to be pronounced as strongly as it would be in a phonetic language.

Text boxes C.1–C.5 provide illustrations of the different sound representations of the five vowel letters, <a>, <e>, <i>, <o> and <u>. It is important to note that most of the sounds that represent these vowel letters include examples of the schwa sound /ə/. We can therefore understand why /ə/ is the most frequent sound in the English language. Another important point to note is that when any of the vowels are followed by the letter <r>, the vowel changes its pronunciation quite radically, usually to an /ɜː/ sound (and in many English accents, the <r> is not pronounced).

Vowel letter <a> and its different sounds

The vowel <a> appears to be the least challenging when it comes to guessing how it should be pronounced. Students quite quickly learn the sound /eɪ/ in words like *table*, *late* or *race*, but they get it mixed up with the /æ/ sound in words such as *apple*, *cat* and *mad*. The schwa sound /ə/ is certainly one of the sounds many students will struggle with.

Text box C.1. Vowel letter <a> and its different sounds

Letter	Sound	Spelling examples
	/æ/	apple, cat, land, mad, travel
	/ɑː/	army, father, calm, car, party
a	/ɔː/	ball, call, chalk, warm
	/ə/	about, brutal, dollar, grammar, sugar
	/eɪ/	able, late, make, race, stable

Vowel letter <e> and its different sounds

The sound representations for the vowel <e> take students from the front sound /iː/ through the middle sound /ɜː/ and right to the back of the mouth with /juː/ and /ə/. No wonder it seems to be the most challenging vowel to guess. 'How can we know whether it is /iː/, /ɜː/ or /juː/?' we were repeatedly asked. 'Use a dictionary if you are not sure,' we often reassured them.

Text box C.2. Vowel letter <e> and its different sounds

Letter	Sound	Spelling examples
	/iː/	be, eve, meet, see, sleep
	/ɪ/	enough, event, eclipse
e	/ɛ/	bed, end, men, let, tell
	/ɜː/	determine, herb, serve
	/ə/	broken, different, even, letter, travel
	/juː/	dew, few, knew, new

Vowel letter <i> and its different sounds

While the pronunciation of the vowel <i> as /ɪ/ in words such as *kiss* or *pick* or /iː/ in words like *ski* or *police* will raise few eyebrows, the <i> in words like *bird*, *skirt* and *sir* requires more careful consideration. It is not an obvious sound for many students.

Text box C.3. Vowel letter <i> and its different sounds

Letter	Sound	Spelling examples
	/ɪ/	kiss, tip, pick, possible
i	/iː/	machine, ski, police, technique
	/aɪ/	ice, find, smile, kite
	/ɜː/	bird, girl, shirt, skirt, sir

Vowel letter <o> and its different sounds

The vowel <o> appears to have a larger number of sound representations than the other vowels: from the open /ɔː/ to the schwa sound /ə/. The letter <o> pronounced /ɒ/ in words such as *bottle*, *model* or *rock* was the most disputed sound among our adult students at the teachers' college in Tanzania. They strongly argued that English natives' unwillingness to pronounce <o> as in /ɔː/ in every word where it is used constitutes a deliberate attempt to confuse non-native speakers. We were explicitly asked to explain why the vowel <o> should be pronounced in so many ways such as /ɜː/, /ɒ/, /əː/ or /ə/ rather than simply as /ɔː/.   Although we referred them to some examples of the vowel <o> in its long form, as in the words *lord*, *more* or *order*, the students did not look convinced.

Text box C.4. Vowel letter <o> and its different sounds

Letter	Sound	Spelling examples
	/əː/	word, work, world, worse
	/əʊ/	both, nose, so, sofa
	/ɔː/	form, lord, normal, order
o	/ɒ/	bottle, gosh, model, rock
	/uː/	broom, do, whose, room
	/ə/	ignorant, offend, pilot

Vowel letter <u> and its different sounds

The suggestion that students would be expected to pronounce the letter <u> as /ʊ/ (short) in the words *full* and *put* or to pronounce it /uː/ (long) in the words *blue or fruit* is pure speculation. However, where there are general principles, such as in the case where <u> followed by <r> becomes /ɜː/ – as in the words *church*, *surprise* and *surrender* – it is possible for students to understand the reason behind the change of sound. Similarly, if it is explained to students that the vowel letter <u> is pronounced /ə/ in unstressed syllables, as in the words *subtract*, *succeed* or *suppose*, but it is pronounced /ʌ/ in stressed syllables, as in the words *supper*, *upper* or *mutter*, then the cloud of misconception can be lifted.

Another good example that can help us understand the difference in the vowel <u> being pronounced /ʌ/ or /ə/ is to consider the noun–verb contrast in the word *suspect*. As a noun, the stress is on the first syllable and thus the <u> is pronounced /ʌ/, but as a verb, the stress shifts to the second syllable. Therefore, the pronunciation of the vowel letter <u> becomes /ə/. Thus, the word *suspect* can be transcribed as /'sʌspekt/ (noun) and /sə'spekt/ (verb). (The symbol /'/ is used to indicate that the next syllable is stressed.)

Letter	Sound	Spelling examples
	/juː/	cute, duty, huge, music, tune, use
	/ʊ/	full, pull, push, put, sugar
u	/uː/	blue, glue, fruit, juice, true
	/ʌ/	cup, cut, duck, gun, study, sun, ugly
	/əː/	burn, church, hurt, surprise
	/ə/	subtract, succeed, suggest, suppose

Table C.1. Vowel letters and their sound representations

Vowel letter <a>		Vowel letter <e>		Vowel letter <i>	
about	/əbaʊt/	bed	/bɛd/	bird	/bəːd/
baby	/beɪbi/	broken	/brəʊkən/	kite	/kaɪt/
bank	/bænk/	event	/ɪvɛnt/	pick	/pɪk/
dark	/daːk/	herb	/həːb/	ski	/skiː/
man	/mæn/	meet	/miːt/		
tall	/tɔːl/	new	/njuː/		

Vowel letter <o>		Vowel letter <u>	
lord	/lɔːd/	blue	/bluː/
nose	/nəʊz/	church	/ʧəːʧ/
pilot	/paɪlət/	cup	/kʌp/
rock	/rɒk/	full	/fʊl/
room	/ruːm/	music	/mjuːzɪk/
work	/wəːk/	suggest	/səʤɛst/

Vowels followed by <w> and their different sounds

When a vowel is followed by <w>, it is not pronounced in the same way as when it is surrounded by other consonants. The following examples show how vowels combined with <w> change their sounds:

Text box C.6. Vowels followed by <w> and their sound changes

Vowel + w	New sound	Examples
e + w	/juː/	dew few mew new pew
a + w	/ɔː/	awful claws law raw saw
o + w	/aʊ/	cow brown now row wow

C2. VOWEL SOUNDS AND THEIR SPELLINGS

The production of vowel sounds has been described in detail in Section C1. Section C2 focuses on the different ways vowel sounds are represented in writing. Compared with consonants, vowel sounds have a larger number of spelling variants. Text boxes C.7–C.26 illustrate how pure vowel sounds and diphthongs are represented in spelling. The following order will be used to introduce the vowel sounds:

a) Front vowels   /iː/, /ɪ/, /e/, /æ/

b) Central vowels   /ɜː/, /ə/, /ʌ/

c) Back vowels   /uː/, /ʊ/, /ɔː/, /ɒ/, /ɑː/

Front vowel sounds

The use of a colon (:) with the /i/ sound – transcribed as /iː/ – is very important. It indicates a long sound, as opposed to the short sound /ɪ/ described in Text box C.8.

Text box C.7. The vowel sound /iː/ and its different spellings

Sound	Letter	Spelling examples
	e	be, these, complete
	ea	beat, cease, leaf, leave, meal, please
	ee	bee, beef, cheese, feed, meet, week
/iː/	i	machine, police, suite, ski
	ie	field, piece, siege
	ei, ey	receive, seize, key
	ey	donkey, honey, monkey, trolley (in final unstressed position, pronounced with short /i/)
	y	city, happy, pretty (unstressed, pronounced with short /i/)

Text box C.8. The vowel sound /ɪ/ and its different spellings

Sound	Letter	Spelling examples
	i	bid, bin, fish, kid, lid, little, tip, rich
/ɪ/	e	England, pretty, wicket
	a	message, orange, surface, village
	y	syllable, symbol

Text box C.9. The vowel sound /e, ɛ/ and its different spellings

Sound	Letter	Spelling examples
	e	bed, end, men, tell, went
/e/, /ɛ/	ea	bread, deaf, head, thread
	a	any, many

Text box C.10. The vowel sound /æ/ and its different spellings

Sound	Letter	Spelling examples
/æ/	a	apple, bag, bat, cat, dad, land, mad, travel
	ai	plaid, plait

Central vowel sounds

The vowel sound /ɜ:/ is generally the result of a vowel being followed by the consonant <r>. A more detailed description of the consonant <r> is offered in Section C4.

Text box C.11. The vowel sound /ɜ:/ and its different spellings

Sound	Letter	Spelling examples
	er	her, fern, perched, perfect, serve
	ur	burn, church, hurt, nurse, purse, surf, turn
/ɜ:/	w + or	word, world, worse, worth
	ir	bird, firm, girl, sir, shirt, skirt
	ear	earth, heard, search
	our	courtesy, journey

The vowel sound /ə/, also known as the *schwa* sound, is the most common sound in English. It is used in *unstressed* syllables or in weak forms. In several contexts, as is the case with /ɜ:/, the schwa sound /ə/ is triggered by the presence of <r>.

Text box C.12. The vowel sound /ə/ and its different spellings

Sound	Letter	Spelling examples
	a	about, affect, woman, Africa, Canada, China
	ar	arrive, grammar, particular
	er	character, mother, teacher, perhaps
/ə/	or	ambassador, doctor, forget, razor
	u	autumn, picture, support, suppose
	ou	ambitious, famous, delicious
	o	offence, contain, ignorant, pilot, photograph

Text box C.13. The vowel sound /ʌ/ and its different spellings

Sound	Letter	Spelling examples
	u	bulb, cup, drug, dull, luck, much, nut, uncle
	o	colour, come, comfort, done, love, mother
/ʌ/	ou	cousin, couple, country, tough, young
	oo	blood, flood
	oe	does

Back vowel sounds

Text box C.14. The vowel sound /u:/ and its different spellings

Sound	Letter	Spelling examples
	oo	broom, food, loose, moon, spoon
	o	do, lose, two, who
/u:/	ew	chew, few, flew, new
	ou	group, soup, through, wound
	u	crucial, June, rude, rule
/ju:/	ew	dew, knew, view
	u, ue	use, duke, due, Tuesday

Text box C.15. The vowel sound /ʊ/ and its different spellings

Sound	Letter	Spelling examples
	oo	book, cook, foot, look, room, wool
	o	wolf, woman
/ʊ/	ou	could, courier, tournament, would
	u	bulletin, cushion, full, push, put

Text box C.16. The vowel sound /ɔ:/ and its different spellings

Sound	Letter	Spelling examples
/ɔ:/	a(l)	ball, call, chalk, talk, walk
	a(r)	quart, war, warn, water
	or, ore	born, form, lord, more, order
	oar, oor	board, door, floor
	ou	bought, thought, ought
	au, aw	daughter, awesome, saw, yawn

Text box C.17. The vowel sound /ɒ/ and its different spellings

Sound	Letter	Spelling examples
/ɒ/	o	bottle, cross, dog, gone, model
	a	want, watch, was, what, yacht
	au	because, cauliflower, sausage
	ou, ow	cough, knowledge

Text box C.18. The vowel sound /ɑ:/ and its different spellings

Sound	Letter	Spelling examples
/ɑ:/	a	ask, bath, father, last, path
	ar	army, car, dark, farm, march, party
	al	calm, half, palm
	au	aunt, laugh
	ear	heart
	er	clerk, Derby, sergeant

Diphthongs and their different spellings

To produce a diphthong sound, the tongue glides from one position (the first vowel sound) to the next (the second vowel sound).

Text box C.19. The diphthong /ɪə/ and its different spellings

Sound	Letter	Spelling examples
/ɪə/	ea	beard, ear, clear, dear, fear, idea, year
	ee	beer, career, cheer, deer, sneer
	er, ere	here, interfere, sincere

Text box C.20. The diphthong /eɪ/ and its different spellings

Sound	Letter	Spelling examples
	a	gate, lake, name, late, male, race
	ai	again, fail, pain, rain, raise, wait
/eɪ/	ay	clay, day, pay, play, way
	ea	break, great, steak
	ei	eight, beige

Text box C.21. The diphthong /eə/ and its different spellings

Sound	Letter	Spelling examples
	ar, are	aware, bare, care, glare, stared
	ear	bear, swear, tear (verb), wear
/eə/	er	there, where
	ai	air, chair, hair, pair

Text box C.22. The diphthong /aɪ/ and its different spellings

Sound	Letter	Spelling examples
	i	child, fine, kite, mine, night, white
	ei, ey	height, eyes, either, neither
/aɪ/	y	buy, cycle, fly, try, type, why
	ie	die, lie, pie, tried

Text box C.23. The diphthong /əʊ/ and its different spellings

Sound	Letter	Spelling examples
	o	cold, home, go, nose, old, wrote
	oa	boat, coal, coach, coast, goat
/əʊ/	ow	blow, flow, glow, low, know, snow
	oe	toe, foe, hoe
	ou	although, boulder, soul, shoulder

Text box C.24. The diphthong /ʊə/ and its different spellings

Sound	Letter	Spelling examples
	oo	boor, moor, poor
/ʊə/	ure	cure, pure, sure, secure
	our	amour, tour, tournament

Text box C.25. The diphthong /ɔɪ/ and its different spellings

Sound	Letter	Spelling examples
/ɔɪ/	oi	avoid, choice, coin, noise, voice
	oy	boy, joy, toy, oyster, annoy

Text box C.26. The diphthong /aʊ/ and its different spellings

Sound	Letter	Spelling examples
/aʊ/	ou	about, doubt, loud, mouth, mouse
	ow	allow, brown, cow, crowd, powder

C3. CONSONANT LETTERS AND THEIR SOUNDS

As a general principle, most English consonants are pronounced as they are written. However, when one considers other factors such as dialects, combinations with other sounds, allophones, aspiration and so on, it is likely that most of these sounds will undergo changes.

In this book, we take the view that *learning is better than guessing*. In other words, students need to spend more time learning/ practising – especially with tricky sounds – rather than attempting to generalise from a few examples. Both consonants and vowels can take different sounds depending on the context in which they occur.

The description of letters and sounds offered in this book shows that several students will find it difficult to guess, for instance, what the vowel <o> will sound like in words such as *bottle*, *do*, *form* or *word* unless they have some basic understanding of the English sound system. Similarly, consonants may be affected by other sounds or by the contextual environment in which they occur. For example, the consonant /r/ appears to trigger a sound change when it occurs after a vowel – the vowel /ɪ/ changes into /ɜː/ when followed by /r/, as seen in the two words *bid* /bɪd/ and *bird* /bɜːd/, while some consonant letters can create new sounds when combined, such as <c> + <h> to produce the sound /tʃ/, as in the word *church*. It is also important to note that some consonants may disappear completely in some contexts. The word *know* is pronounced /nəʊ/ without the <k>, and, equally, the word *debt* is pronounced /dɛt/ without the <b>. See Appendix 4 for more examples of silent letters.

In this book, we will limit our discussion to three consonant letters: <c>, <g> and <r>. First, here is the full list of consonant letters and their regular sounds:

Text box C.27. The consonant letters and their sounds

Letter	Sound	Examples
p	/p/	pen, pepper, pop
b	/b/	ball, rubber, bulb
c	/k/	cat, account, ache, quick
k	/k/	karate, turkey, kite, kick
g	/g/	go, begin, egg, ghost
t	/t/	top, cattle, market
d	/d/	desk, middle, did
f	/f/	food, offer, laugh
v	/v/	vary, navy, dove
s	/s/	sit, lesson, loss, science
s	/z/	was, scissors
z	/z/	zoo, puzzle, buzz
m	/m/	man, immense, autumn
n	/n/	nose, nanny, often, oven
l	/l/	let, balloon, pool
r	/r/	red, marry, four and a half (linked with vowel)
h	/h/	hot, behave
j	/dʒ/	jacket, jam, enjoy
w	/w/	walk, always, wow

The consonant letter <c> and its sounds

We will consider, for the sake of illustration, the consonant letters <c> and <g>. These two consonant letters do not have unique sounds, even when followed by the same vowel letter.

The first case is that of the consonant <c>. The following examples illustrate the different pronunciations of the letter in initial position.

When the initial consonant <c> is followed by the vowel <a>, <c> is generally pronounced as /k/, except in a few examples of words of foreign origin.

Examples

cable, café, cake, calendar, campus, candle, capital, card, catalogue, cave

Exceptions

The words listed all have an <e> after the <a>.

caecilian	/sɪˈsɪlɪən/
caecum	/ˈsɪkəm/
Caesar	/ˈsiːzə/
caesarean	/sɪˈzeːrɪən/
caesium	/ˈsiːzɪəm/

When the initial consonant <c> is followed by the vowel <e>, <c> is usually pronounced as /s/, except for a few borrowed words.

Examples

ceiling, celery, celebrate, cellphone, centigrade, centre, century, census, cereal, certificate

Exceptions

ceilidh	/keɪli/
celt	/kɛlt/
Celtic	/kɛltɪk/
Cerenkov (radiation)	/ʧərɛŋkəf/
ceteris	/ketərɪs/

When the initial consonant <c> is followed by the vowel <i>, it is pronounced as /s/, except for a few coined words.

Examples

cinema, cigarette, cinnamon, circle, circus, circumstance, citation, citizen, city, civilisation

Exceptions

ciao	/ʧaʊ/
cicerone	/ʧɪʧə'rəʊni/

The letter <c> followed by the letter <o>

When the initial consonant <c> is followed by the vowel <o>, it is usually pronounced as /k/, except for most imported words.

Examples

coach, coconut, colleague, colour, comedy, comment, compliment, condition, connection, corruption

Exceptions

coelacanth	/'siːləkanθ/
coeliac	/'siːlɪak/
coelom	/'siːləm/
coelostat	/'siːləstat/
coenobite	/'siːnəʊbaɪt/

The letter <c> followed by the letter <u>

When the initial consonant <c> is followed by the vowel <u>, <c> can be pronounced either as /k/ or /kj/.

Examples

/k/: cuddle, culprit, cultivate, culture, cup

/kj/: cube, curable, curiosity, cure, cute

The letter <c> followed by the letter <y>

As is the case with <c> followed by <i>, when the consonant <c> is followed by the semi-vowel <y>, it is pronounced as /s/.

Examples

cycle, cyclone, cylinder, cynical, cytoplasm

Exceptions

The consonant letter <c> followed by <y> is /kɪ/ in words of Welsh origin, as in:

Cymric (or Kymric) and Cymry (or Kymry)

Text box C.28. The consonant letter <c> and its different sounds

Letter	Followed by	Pronounced	Examples
	a	/k/	café, campus, cave
	e	/s/	ceiling, centigrade, certificate
	i	/s/	cinema, circle, citizen
c	o	/k/	coach, comment, corruption
	u	/k/ or /kj/	cuddle, cup, cube, cure
	y	/s/	cycle, cylinder, cytoplasm

The consonant letter <g> and its sounds

The second example is that of the consonant letter <g>. Overall, the letter is pronounced either as /g/ or as /dʒ/ in initial position, but there are variations.

The letter <g> followed by the letter <a>

When the initial consonant <g> is followed by the vowel <a>, it is usually pronounced as /g/.

Examples

galaxy, gallery, gamble, garage, garden, garlic, gasoline, gastronomy, gatekeeper, gazelle

The letter <g> followed by the letter <e>

When the initial consonant <g> is followed by the vowel <e>, it is usually pronounced as /dʒ/, but in a few cases, the sound /g/ is maintained.

Examples

/dʒ/: gender, gentle, general, geography, gesture, genius, genetics, genuine

/g/: gear, geek, geezer, get

When the initial consonant <g> is followed by the vowel <i>, <g> may be pronounced either as /g/ or as /dʒ/.

Examples

/dʒ/: giant, ginger, giraffe, gigantic, ginseng

/g/: gibbon, gift, giggle, girl, give

Whenever the initial consonant <g> is followed by the vowel <o>, <g> is pronounced as /g/.

Examples

goal, gobsmacked, godfather, gold, goldfish, goodbye, goose, gourmet, government

There are two categories of words under this combination. The first is made up of words which have the structure <g> and <u> + consonant, and the second is made of words which follow the structure <g> and <u> + vowel. Although the pronunciation of the <g> in most of these words as /g/ is the same, the difference in structure is important when spelling the words.

Examples

<g> and <u> + consonant: gulf, gum, gullet, gun, gutter

<g> and <u> + vowel: guard, guava, guest, guitar, guilty

Whenever the initial consonant <g> is followed by the semi-vowel <y>, <g> is pronounced as /dʒ/. There are not many words in this category in English.

Examples

gymnasium/gymnast, gypsy, gymslip, gyroscope

Exception

gynaecology

Text box C.29. The consonant letter <g> and its different sounds

Letter	Followed by	Pronounced	Examples
	a	/g/	galaxy, garden, gazelle
	e	/dʒ/ or /ʒ/	geography, genetics // genre
g	i	/g/ or /dʒ/	gift, give // giant, giraffe
	o	/g/	goal, goodbye, government
	u	/g/	gulf, gutter, guard, guitar
	y	/dʒ/	gymnastics, gypsy

The consonant letter <r> and its sounds

The pronunciation of the consonant <r> is possibly one of the most challenging sounds in the English sound system for students learning English. As students ourselves, we have struggled to master the /r/ sound, especially when it causes a change to the preceding vowel. The /r/ sound is pronounced differently in initial position than in medial or final positions.

The /r/ sound in initial position

The /r/ sound is fully voiced in initial position and when followed by a vowel, as in:

rabbit	radio	rain	razor
read	record	report	respect
rich	ride	right	ring
road	robot	rock	rose
rude	rumba	runner	Russia

The /r/ sound in second position – after a consonant

The /r/ is also fully voiced when it occurs after a voiced consonant; but it is devoiced after a voiceless consonant. The examples highlight the difference:

brake	bread	brown	bright
dream	dress	drink	drove
grace	green	grind	ground
crash	cream	crop	crowd
frame	French	friend	fruit

| prayer | present | progress | prudent |
| train | tree | trip | trouble |

The /r/ sound in third position – preceded by two consonants

The /r/ is somewhat devoiced when /r/ is part of a three-consonant cluster starting with /s/:

| scramble | scream | scribe | shrink |
| spring | strange | street | strength |

The pronunciation of most of these clusters starts with a long /s/ sound before moving to the appropriate consonant. Words starting with <s> appear to be the most common type of three-consonant clusters in English (see also Section B5 on consonant clusters).

The /r/ sound in medial position – surrounded by consonants and vowels

The /r/ is devoiced in medial position when preceded by another consonant, as in:

address	across	contract	country
describe	district	doctrine	extra
fabric	hundred	hungry	improve
increase	obstruction	secretary	surprise

The sound /r/ is fully voiced when surrounded by vowel sounds (intervocalic):

accurate	arrive	bureau	correct
dictionary	during	error	forest
hero	hurry	marriage	memory
narrative	operation	parents	separate
sorry	story	tomorrow	victory

However, in some medial positions, when /r/ is preceded by a vowel sound and followed by a consonant, it may trigger a change in the vowel sound, typically turning it into /ɜːl/, as in these examples:

bird	circle	girl	shirt
alert	herb	perk	serve
word	work	world	worse
burn	curse	church	hurt

The /r/ sound in final position

In final position, the /r/ sound is generally not pronounced; it completely disappears. However, in many cases, its presence at the end of the word triggers a change of the vowel into a schwa sound /ə/. Here are a few examples of both possibilities:

a) the /r/ sound completely disappears, as in:

car	fair	four
scar	stair	there

b) in most cases, when the /r/ sound is in final position and is preceded by a vowel, it triggers a change of the vowel into a schwa sound /ə/. This phenomenon also occurs with other combinations. Here are some examples:

Table C.2. The sound /r/ in final position

-ar	-er	-or	-ure
altar	answer	actor	closure
alveolar	brother	author	figure
calendar	chapter	doctor	future
collar	clever	error	gesture
dollar	danger	major	mixture
familiar	daughter	minor	nature
grammar	father	motor	pasture
molar	gender	razor	picture
popular	hammer	sailor	pleasure
regular	mother	splendour	pressure
scholar	never	senior	puncture
singular	paper	terror	sculpture
spectacular	shelter	tailor	stature
solar	sister	traitor	structure
sugar	spider	tutor	texture

Other uses of /r/ at the end of words with the schwa sound /ə/ include:

ear: fear, clear, dear, nuclear, spear, tear

oor/our/ower: poor, our, tour, power, tower

In some cases, the /r/ in final position is, however, pronounced when it is followed by a word starting with a vowel sound. This process is known as *linking r*.

> You're *better off* staying indoors.
> Jacob likes his new *pair of* shoes.
> There were *four or* five people in the room.
> *Where is* the book? *Here it* is.
> The village is still *far away*.

C4. SILENT LETTERS: NOT PRONOUNCED

Silent letters are present in the written form of the word but are not pronounced. This is particularly true with the letter <r> in final position, as described in Section C3. There are, however, many other letters that can be silent in certain contexts. It is generally not easy to guess these if you are learning English. The examples in Table C.3 illustrate some of those letters and where they can be silent. Some more examples of silent letters can be found in Appendix 4.

Table C.3. Silent letters

Word	How it is said	Word	How it is said	Letter omitted
autumn	/ɔːtəm/	hymn	/hɪm/	n
climb	/klaɪm/	lamb	/læm/	b
cupboard	/kʌbəd/	psychology	/saɪkɒlədʒi/	p
daughter	/dɔːtə/	light	/laɪt/	gh
honest	/ɒnɪst/	hour	/aʊə/	h
iron	/aɪən/	lord	/lɔːd/	r
island	/aɪlənd/	isle	/aɪl/	s
grandfather	/grænfaːðə/	Wednesday	/wenzdi/	d
knife	/naɪf/	know	/nəʊ/	k
listen	/lɪsən/	often	/ɒfən/	t
talk	/tɔːk/	calm	/kaːm/	l
science	/saɪəns/	muscle	/mʌsəl/	c
sign	/saɪn/	foreign	/fɒrɪn/	g
sword	/sɔːd/	two	/tuː/	w
hope	/həʊp/	write	/raɪt/	e
guest	/gest/	guitar	/gɪtaː/	u

SECTION C ACTIVITIES

ACTIVITY C1. LETTERS AND SOUNDS

All these words have an <a> vowel letter in them. Highlight or underline the vowel <a> in the words.

about   baby   bank

dark   man   tall

Transcribe phonemically the words to reveal the differences. An example has been given for you:

bank   /bænk/   about   _____

baby   _____   dark   _____

man   _____   tall   _____

ACTIVITY C2. DIFFERENT VOWELS: SHORT, LONG OR DIPHTHONG

Read aloud these 12 words, paying particular attention to the vowel sound in each word.

bed   car   care   hit

face   ball   cold   could

kite   cut   church   boy

Decide whether the vowel in the word is short, long or a diphthong. List the words next to the correct description. One example has been given for you.

Short vowel

_____ _____ _____ _____

Long vowel   car

_____ _____ _____ _____

Diphthong

_____ _____ _____ _____

ACTIVITY C3. SONORITY OF THE /r/ SOUND

Read the following words as many times as you wish. Work out the sonority of the /r/ sound. Decide whether the sound /r/ is <u>fully voiced</u>, <u>voiced</u> or <u>devoiced</u>. Write the words under the correct column. An example has been given for you.

arrive	contract	bright	spring	red
drink	robot	frog	correct	street
rain	drain	strange	hundred	dream

/r/ **fully voiced**	/r/ **voiced**	/r/ **devoiced**
rain	bright	strange
_____	_____	_____
_____	_____	_____
_____	_____	_____
_____	_____	_____
_____	_____	_____

ACTIVITY C4. /r/ SOUND IN MEDIAL POSITION

When the /r/ sound is used in medial position and it is preceded by one of the vowels <i, e, o, u>, the presence of the /r/ may trigger the change of the vowel sound into an /ɜ:/ sound.

Now find three examples for each vowel with the /r/ sound in medial position. An example has been given for you.

<i>   shirt

_____   _____   _____

<e>

_____   _____   _____

<o>

_____   _____   _____

<u>

_____   _____   _____

ACTIVITY C5. SCHWA SOUND /ə/ IN FINAL POSITION

Find three more examples for each word ending (-ar, -er, -ear, -or and -ure) with a schwa /ə/ sound.

calendar

_____   _____   _____

chapter

_____   _____   _____

clear

_____   _____   _____

doctor

_____   _____   _____

nature

_____   _____   _____

ACTIVITY C6. SILENT LETTERS

Practise saying aloud the words in the left column. Is there any difference between the spoken and written words? Which letters are *not* pronounced?

Transcribe the words phonemically (in the middle column). Write down in the right column the letters which are not pronounced. One example has been given for you.

Word	Transcription	Silent letter
answer	/ɑːnsə/	w/r
climb		
cupboard		
daughter		
island		
Wednesday		

D. STRESS WITHIN ROOT WORDS

Section D explains two concepts which are central to this book: word and syllable. We will discuss them through three main questions:

1) What is meant by the concept of *word*?
2) What is the difference between a word and a syllable?
3) When does a word need to be marked with stress?

A word can be described as 'a single meaningful unit of (spoken or written) language'. This definition implies there are two aspects to the concept *word*: (1) the form and structure of the concept (its morphology), and (2) the way it is said (its phonological representation). In other words, there is a difference between the written and spoken forms of words in English. This is explained in detail in this section.

Unlike a word, a syllable is a unit of speech. To be more precise, a syllable:

- is a unit of speech having a vowel sound as its central element;
- can be a vowel which may or may not be surrounded by consonants;
- can be a word or part of a word.

Section D therefore opens with a description of the distinction between a word and a syllable.

D1. WORDS AND SYLLABLES

The words *come, sheep, market* and *computer* have the following spoken forms (or phonological representations):

Table D.1. Difference between written word and spoken word

Written word	Spoken form of the word
come	/kʌm/
sheep	/ʃiːp/
market	/mɑːkɪt/
computer	/kəmpjutə/

The next step is to be able to determine the number of syllables in each of the four spoken words. When we apply the definition of a syllable to the spoken forms of the words, we realise that the words /kʌm/ and /ʃiːp/ each have one vowel sound when they are spoken, whereas the words /mɑːkɪt/ and /kəmpjutə/ have two and three vowel sounds respectively. We can safely conclude that the first two words, /kʌm/ and /ʃiːp/, have one syllable each, while the third one, /mɑːkɪt/, has two syllables. However, in the last word, /kəmpjutə/, one can hear three syllables.

In short, in single-syllable words, such as the word *come*, one can hear only one vowel sound, /ʌ/, but the word *market* has two vowel sounds, /ɑː/ and /ɪ/. Thus, the word *come* has one syllable while the word *market* has two. In other words, *syllables are determined by the number of vowel sounds one hears and NOT by the number of letters used to spell the word.*

To help understand the role of vowels as central to the concept of syllable, the description of the four words *come*, *sheep*, *market* and *computer* is presented here in a different format to highlight the difference between vowel letters (written) and vowel sounds (spoken):

Table D.2. The difference between vowel letters and vowel sounds

Word	Vowel letter	Spoken form	Vowel sound	Number of syllables
come	two vowel letters <o, e>	/kʌm/	One vowel sound /ʌ/	1
sheep	two vowel letters <e, e>	/ʃiːp/	One vowel sound /iː/	1
market	two vowel letters <a, e>	/ˈmɑːkɪt/	two vowel sounds /ɑː/, /ɪ/	2
computer	three vowel letters <o, u, e>	/kəmˈpjutə/	three vowel sounds /ə/, /ju/, /ə/	3

D2. WORD STRESS

When a word has two syllables or more, as in the words *market* and *computer*, that word must be marked with *stress* to determine its meaning. The *stressed syllable* is pronounced *louder*, *higher* and *longer* than the unstressed syllables. *Market* has the stress on the first syllable, /ˈmɑːkɪt/, whereas *computer* has its stress on the second syllable, /kəmˈpjuːtə/.

Similarly, the difference between **permit** (noun) and per**mit** (verb) is made clear by the position of the stress within these two words – here marked in bold letters. We should remind ourselves, as explained above, that the number of syllables is determined by the number of *vowel sounds* one hears, and not by the number of letters in the word. Stress is particularly important in differentiating the meanings between word-class words, like *permit* (noun) and *permit* (verb), to ensure that the correct meaning is communicated effectively.

Whenever words (with two or more syllables) are marked with stress, it implies that another part or parts of those words are unstressed. The word *market*, /ˈmɑːkɪt/, has the stress on the first syllable while the second syllable is unstressed. Similarly, the word *computer*, /kəmˈpjuːtə/, has the stress on the second syllable, with the first and third syllables unstressed. The contrast *stressed–unstressed* is an important feature in connected speech, as described later in Section G.

When students initially learn to correctly pronounce two-syllable words, they should be able to expand their knowledge to longer words like *computer*. The more students practise using stress, the better they will understand the difference between *stressed* and *unstressed* syllables. Correctly marking stress within multiple-syllable words is a crucial step towards achieving accurate pronunciation.

D3. ONE-SYLLABLE WORDS (MONOSYLLABIC)

English words with one syllable can have different structures

> **Consonant(s) + Vowel + Consonant(s) (CVC)**, as in the words *bet*, *cat*, *gold*, *must*: these types of syllables are known as closed syllables. However, it is important to note that 'C' can stand for more than one consonant, as

in the examples *block, string* or *strength*. These words have one vowel sound and are therefore described as one-syllable words.

Consonant(s) + Vowel (CV), as in words like *be, go, key, to*: these types of syllables are known as *open* syllables. Note that the spelling may contain two vowels, as in the words *bee, due* or *shoe*.

Vowel + Consonant(s) (VC), as in the words *ask, ill, of, us*: these types of syllables are also called *closed* syllables.

Vowel on its own (V), as in words like *a* (article) and *I* (pronoun). These syllables made up of a single vowel are known as *minimal* syllables.

A one-syllable word can take one of the following structures:

Table D.3. Possible syllable structures

Spoken word	Onset	Nucleus	Coda	Type of syllable
/bʌs/	consonant /b/	vowel /ʌ/	consonant /s/	closed
/æt/	-	vowel /æ/	consonant /t/	closed
/gəʊ/	consonant /g/	vowel /əʊ/	-	open

To help students understand the concepts of both *syllable* and *stress*, we will make use of examples of words taken from everyday language. Each word has been transcribed phonemically to allow students to visualise the exact number of vowel sounds and therefore make it easier to determine the number of syllables in that word. Here are examples of one-syllable words from everyday vocabulary:

Note: a more extensive list of randomly selected, commonly used words is in Appendix 5.

Table D.4. Single-syllable words: animals, birds and classroom objects

Animals		Birds		Classroom objects	
cat	/kæt/	cock	/kɒk/	book	/bʊk/
cow	/kaʊ/	dove	/dʌv/	break	/breɪk/
dog	/dɒg/	hen	/hɛn/	desk	/dɛsk/
horse	/hɔːs/	goose	/guːs/	pen	/pɛn/
sheep	/ʃiːp/	swan	/swɒn/	work	/wɜːk/

Table D.5. Single-syllable words: clothing, family members, and food and drink

Clothing items		Family members		Food and drink	
blouse	/blaʊz/	aunt	/ɑːnt/	bread	/brɛd/
dress	/drɛs/	child	/tʃaɪld/	cheese	/tʃiːz/
coat	/kəʊt/	girl	/gɜːl/	fish	/fɪʃ/
shirt	/ʃɜːt/	son	/sʌn/	milk	/mɪlk/
shorts	/ʃɔːts/	wife	/waɪf/	tea	/tiː/

Table D.6. Single-syllable words: fruits, furniture, and games and sports

Fruits		Furniture		Games and sports	
grape	/greɪp/	bed	/bɛd/	cards	/kɑːdz/
nut	/nʌt/	chair	/tʃɛə/	chess	/tʃɛs/
peach	/piːtʃ/	seat	/siːt/	darts	/dɑːts/
pear	/pɛə/	shelf	/ʃɛlf/	draughts	/drɑːfts/
plum	/plʌm/	stool	/stuːl/	golf	/gɒlf/

Table D.7. Single-syllable words: insects, kitchen and shopping

Insects		Kitchen		Shopping	
ant	/ænt/	cup	/kʌp/	buy	/baɪ/
bee	/biː/	fork	/fɔːk/	goods	/gʊdz/
bug	/bʌg/	glass	/glɑːs/	pay	/peɪ/
fly	/flaɪ/	knife	/naɪf/	purse	/pɜːs/
louse	/laʊs/	plate	/pleɪt/	shop	/ʃɒp/

D4. TWO-SYLLABLE WORDS (DISYLLABIC)

When a word has more than one syllable, not all the syllables are pronounced with the same degree of force. One syllable will carry the primary stress (the strong syllable) and the other will have secondary stress (the weak syllable). The *primary stressed syllable* is pronounced *louder*, *higher* and *longer*.

Marking stress in two-syllable nouns and adjectives

Two-syllable nouns and adjectives seem to follow similar tendencies when it comes to stress placement. It is important to note that only one syllable is stressed, not both. Most two-syllable nouns and adjectives in English have their stress on the first syllable, except where this syllable is weak. Syllables containing the vowel sound /ə/ are usually unstressed and therefore weak.

Nouns with a strong syllable at the beginning:

> city, lesson, market, picture, table – all have the stress on the first syllable

Nouns with a weak syllable at the beginning:

> address, event, hotel, mistake, today – all have the stress on the second syllable

Adjectives with a strong syllable in initial position:

> clever, famous, happy, lazy, pleasant – all have their stress on the first syllable

Adjectives with a weak syllable at the beginning:

> afraid, mature, polite, obese, unique – all have their stress on the second syllable

Although these are not firm rules, the general tendency is very clear in these examples. However, students must remember that there are many exceptions to this tendency. The examples of two-syllable words given in Tables D8–D.11 are mainly made up of nouns. Thus, according to the general tendency described above, most of them carry stress on the first syllable.

Table D.8. Two-syllable words: animals, birds and classroom objects

Animals		Birds		Classroom objects	
camel	/ˈkæməl/	parrot	/ˈpærət/	lesson	/ˈlɛsən/
donkey	/ˈdɒŋki/	penguin	/ˈpɛŋgwɪn/	paper	/ˈpeɪpə/
leopard	/ˈlɛpəd/	pigeon	/ˈpɪdʒɪn/	pencil	/ˈpɛnsəl/
tiger	/ˈtaɪgə/	pheasant	/ˈfɛzənt/	student	/ˈstjuːdənt/
zebra	/ˈzɛbrə/	turkey	/ˈtɜːki/	teacher	/ˈtiːʧə/

Table D.9. Two-syllable words: clothing, family members, and food and drink

Clothing items		Family members		Food and drink	
jacket	/ˈdʒækɪt/	brother	/ˈbrʌðə/	chicken	/ˈʧɪkɪn/
jumper	/ˈdʒʌmpə/	daughter	/ˈdɔːtə/	coffee	/ˈkɒfi/
handbag	/ˈhændbæg/	father	/ˈfɑːðə/	dinner	/ˈdɪnə/
raincoat	/ˈreɪnkəʊt/	mother	/ˈmʌðə/	sandwich	/ˈsændwɪʧ/
trousers	/ˈtraʊzəz	sister	/ˈsɪstə/	water	/ˈwɔːtə/

Table D.10. Two-syllable words: fruits, furniture, and games and sports

Fruits		Furniture		Games and sports	
apple	/ˈæpəl/	armchair	/ˈɑːmtʃɛə/	boxing	/ˈbɒksɪŋ/
grapefruit	/ˈgreɪpfruːt/	bureau	/ˈbjuərəʊ/	cricket	/ˈkrɪkɪt/
lemon	/ˈlɛmən/	cooker	/ˈkʊkə/	football	/ˈfʊtbɔːl/
mango	/ˈmæŋgəʊ/	cupboard	/ˈkʌbəd/	swimming	/ˈswɪmɪŋ/
orange	/ˈɒrɪndʒ/	table	/ˈteɪbəl/	tennis	/ˈtɛnɪs/

Table D.11. Two-syllable words: insects, kitchen and shopping

Insects		Kitchen		Shopping	
beetle	/ˈbiːtəl/	blender	/ˈblɛndə/	banknote	/ˈbæŋknəʊt/
cockroach	/ˈkɒkrəʊtʃ/	cooker	/ˈkʊkə/	money	/ˈmʌni/
cricket	/ˈkrɪkɪt/	kettle	/ˈkɛtəl/	purchase	/ˈpɜːtʃɪs/
spider	/ˈspaɪdə/	saucepan	/ˈsɔːspən/	saving	/ˈseɪvɪŋ/
termite	/ˈtɜːmaɪt/	steamer	/ˈstiːmə/	wallet	/ˈwɒlɪt/

Marking stress within two-syllable verbs

The general tendency for marking stress in two-syllable verbs is the opposite of what was described earlier when dealing with nouns and adjectives. Here, the main tendency is to stress the second syllable rather than the first. This is because many two-syllable verbs have weak syllables in initial position, that is, syllables containing the vowel sounds /ə, ɪ, i, u/.

Verbs with weak syllables at the beginning:

> *accept, begin, decide, forget, protect* – all have their stress on the second syllable

Verbs with strong syllables at the beginning:

> *argue, cancel, enter, marry, promise* – all have their stress on the first syllable

These general tendencies can be easily applied when we learn to transcribe the words phonemically and understand the difference between weak and strong syllables.

It is understandable that non-native speakers are likely to find the shift of stress that characterises English pronunciation a challenging exercise. In fact, marking stress in French seems to be relatively consistent: usually the last syllable is stressed. Let us take an example:

Monsieur Justin viendra demain dans l'après midi

In this sentence, composed mainly of two-syllable nouns (and a verb), the position of stress is very consistent: it is always on the second syllable. Such consistency does not occur in English, as described in the next section.

Marking stress within noun–verb pairs

There are, in English, pairs of two-syllable words with the same spellings. Although spelt in an identical way, these pairs of words carry different meanings depending on the position of the stress. In these noun–verb pairs, the nouns have their stress on the first syllable while the verbs have their stress on the second syllable. The general tendency described under the difference between 'strong' and 'weak' syllables is also seen through the change of vowel sound, for instance, from /'kɒntrɑːst/ (noun) to /kən'trɑːst/ (verb). Here are some more examples:

Table D.12. Stress within noun–verb pairs

Noun		Verb	
Word	Spoken form	Word	Spoken form
contest	/'kɒntɛst/	contest	/kən'tɛst/
contract	/'kɒntrækt/	contract	/kən'trækt/
contrast	/'kɒntrɑːst/	contrast	/kən'trɑːst/
escort	/'ɛskɔːt/	escort	/ɪs'kɔːt/
export	/'ɛkspɔːt/	export	/ɪ'kspɔːt/
import	/'ɪmpɔːt/	import	/ɪm'pɔːt/
object	/'ɒbdʒɪkt/	object	/əb'dʒɛkt/
permit	/'pɜːmɪt/	permit	/pə'mɪt/
present	/'prɛzənt/	present	/prɪ'zɛnt/
protest	/'prəʊtɛst/	protest	/prə'tɛst/
record	/'rɛkɔːd/	record	/rɪ'kɔːd/
transport	/'trænspɔːt/	transport	/træns'pɔːt/

D5. MULTIPLE-SYLLABLE WORDS (POLYSYLLABIC)

Our description of stress placement in two-syllable words has offered some indication that stress patterns are not always fixed in English. There are both exceptions and variations. Such changes in stress patterns become even more complex as the number of syllables in a word increases.

However, Section D4 shows that, by considering several features, one can positively predict tendencies in stress placement. Features such as the grammatical class of a word (noun or verb) and the nature of its syllables (strong or weak) play an important role in determining the position of stress. We can reasonably conclude that, broadly speaking, similar features are used to help decide the position of stress in words with up to three syllables. However, when words have more than three syllables, such well-defined tendencies are not evident.

To start with, there exist in English a few words – with more than two syllables – that do not follow any given tendency, that is, the position of stress within them is not fixed. Speakers of English can shift the position of stress within the following words without affecting their meanings:

Table D.13. Multiple-syllable words with a shift of stress position

Word	Stress position 1	Stress position 2
controversy	/ˈkɒntrəvɜːsi/	/kənˈtrɒvəsi/
formidable	/ˈfɔːmɪdəbl/	/fəˈmɪdəbl/
kilometre	/ˈkɪləmiːtə/	/kɪˈlɒmɪtə/
television	/ˈtɛlɪvɪʒən/	/tɛlɪˈvɪʒən/

Marking stress within multiple-syllable words

As described at the beginning of this section, stress placement within longer words is likely to present more challenges to students, especially for beginners. The placement of stress within multiple-syllable words does not seem to follow any rules or tendencies. However, in several cases, researchers tend to agree on certain diagnostic features, including those already mentioned, such as:

a) the grammatical category of the word (noun, verb or adjective);

b) the nature of the syllables in the word (strong or weak);

c) whether or not there are affixes attached to the word.

The first two features, (a) and (b), have been extensively referred to in the sections above in the description of two-syllable words. Let us also reiterate the view that when a word has two or more syllables, the stress needs to be accurately placed to determine its meaning. In this section, we would like to start with the first two features when considering stress placement within multiple-syllable words. Feature (c), however, brings in another challenge: we need to distinguish between root words and words with affixes. Words with affixes will be discussed in the next section. Our focus here will be on root words.

Root words are those words that can stand alone. Most examples (see Section D4) of two-syllable words are root words. In the next section, the distinction between root words and words with affixes will become clearer when we discuss how the addition of an affix may change the position of stress.

Root words can be nouns, verbs or adjectives. Adverbs are generally the result of adding an affix. Thus, we will not include adverbs as root words in the following examples.

Root nouns with a strong syllable at the beginning:

> *anecdote, antelope, camera, history, telephone* – all have their stress on the first syllable

Root nouns with a strong syllable in the middle:

> *complexion, encounter, potato, tobacco, tomato* – all have their stress on the second syllable

Root nouns with a strong syllable at the end:

> *avocado, afternoon, cigarette, kangaroo* – all have their stress on the third syllable

Root verbs with a strong syllable at the beginning:

> *advocate, emigrate, organise, sympathise, westernise* – all have their stress on the first syllable

Root verbs with a strong syllable in the middle:

> *astonish, develop, examine, imagine, resemble* – all have their stress on the second syllable

Root verbs with a strong syllable at the end:

entertain, recommend, overtake, understand – all have their
stress on the third syllable

Root adjectives with a strong syllable at the beginning:

dangerous, difficult, necessary, possible – all have their
stress on the first syllable

Root adjectives with a strong syllable in the middle:

excessive, explicit, impatient – all have their stress on the
second syllable

For most students of English, the important thing in learning a
theory is to be able to apply it in real life. So the different tendencies
in stress placement described throughout the book need to be
seen in practice. Just as we did with two-syllable words, stress
placement within multiple-syllable words will be made as accessible
as possible to students. That is why, once more, we are going to
refer to commonly used words to illustrate the placement of stress
within multiple-syllable words.

Table D.14. Multiple-syllable words: animals and birds

Animals		Birds	
buffalo	/ˈbʌfələʊ/	albatross	/ˈalbətrɒs/
elephant	/ˈɛlɪfənt/	flamingo	/fləˈmɪŋgəʊ/
kangaroo	/ˈkæŋgəruː/	hummingbird	/ˈhʌmɪnbɜːd/
rhinoceros	/raɪˈnɒsərəs/	kingfisher	/ˈkɪŋfɪʃə/
hippopotamus	/hɪpəˈpɒtəməs/	nightingale	/ˈnaɪtɪŋgeɪl/

Table D.15. Multiple-syllable words: classroom objects and clothing

Classroom objects		Clothing items	
computer	/kəmˈpjuːtə/	overcoat	/ˈəʊvəkəʊt/
detention	/dɪˈtenʃən/	pyjamas	/pəˈdʒɑːməz/
handwriting	/ˈhændraɪtɪŋ/	umbrella	/ʌmˈbrɛlə/
calculator	/ˈkælkjʊleɪtə/	underwear	/ˈʌndəweə/
dictionary	/ˈdɪkʃənəri/	uniform	/ˈjuːnɪfɔːm/

Table D.16. Multiple-syllable words: family members and food and drink

Family members		Food and drink	
adolescent	/ædəˈlɛsənt/	chocolate	/ˈtʃɒkəlɪt/
ancestor	/ˈænsestə/	lemonade	/lɛməˈneɪd/
grandfather	/ˈgrænfɑːðə/	margarine	/ˈmɑːdʒəriːn/
stepbrother	/ˈstɛpbrʌðə/	pepperoni	/pɛpəˈrəʊni/
teenager	/ˈtiːneɪdʒə/	semolina	/sɛməˈliːnə/

Table D.17. Multiple-syllable words: fruits and furniture

Fruits		Furniture	
avocado	/ævəˈkɑːdəʊ/	chandelier	/ʃændɪˈlɪə/
banana	/bəˈnɑːnə/	loudspeaker	/laʊdˈspiːkə/
coconut	/ˈkəʊkənʌt/	typewriter	/ˈtaɪpraɪtə/
pineapple	/ˈpaɪnæpəl/	television	/tɛlɪˈvɪʒən/
strawberry	/ˈstrɔːbəri/	wardrobe	/wɔːdrəʊb/

Table D.18. Multiple-syllable words: games, sports and insects

Games and sports		Insects	
aerobatics	/ɛərəʊˈbætɪks/	bumblebee	/ˈbʌmbəlbiː/
basketball	/ˈbɑːskɪtbɔːl/	butterfly	/ˈbʌtəflaɪ/
gymnastics	/dʒɪmˈnæstɪks/	grasshopper	/ˈgrɑːshɒpə/
marathon	/ˈmærəθən/	ladybird	/ˈleɪdɪbɜːd/
weightlifting	/ˈweɪtlɪftɪŋ/	mosquito	/məsˈkiːtəʊ/

Table D.19. Multiple-syllable words: kitchen and shopping

Kitchen		Shopping	
casserole	/ˈkæsərəʊl/	customer	/ˈkʌstəmə/
dishwasher	/ˈdɪʃwɒʃə/	newspaper	/ˈnjuːzpeɪpə/
microwave	/ˈmaɪkrəʊweɪv/	reduction	/rɪˈdʌkʃən/
refrigerator	/rɪˈfrɪdʒəreɪtə/	shopkeeper	/ˈʃɒpkiːpə/
thermometer	/θəˈmɒmɪtə/	supermarket	/ˈsuːpəmaːkɪt/

SECTION D ACTIVITIES

Change these phonemic transcriptions into words. An example has been given for you.

/ˈænsestə/   ancestor

/ˈbæŋknəʊt/

/ˈbʌfələʊ/

/ˈkɒkrəʊtʃ/

/ˈmɑːdʒəriːn/

/ˈtiːneɪdʒə/

/pəˈdʒɑːməz/

Where is the stress placed within these three popular words? Mark the syllable with the stress on it.

controversy

kilometre

television

ACTIVITY D3. PHONEMIC TRANSCRIPTION, SYLLABLES AND STRESS PLACEMENT

Transcribe phonemically these words; determine the number of syllables in each of them and mark the stress in the correct position within the word. One example has been done for you.

Word	Transcription	No. of syllables	Stress position
detention	/dɪˈtenʃən/	3	Second syllable
avocado			
computer			
dictionary			
lemonade			
pineapple			
supermarket			

ACTIVITY D4. WORDS, SYLLABLES AND STRESS PLACEMENT

When a word has two syllables or more, it carries stress. For illustration purposes, bar charts are used to represent the number of syllables in a word. Two-bar charts represent words with two syllables, three-bar charts represent words with three syllables and so on. A 'tall' bar represents the syllable with the stress. The stress can therefore fall on the first, the second or the third syllable.

Find at least <u>two more words</u> to fill in each column. An example has been given for you for each bar chart.

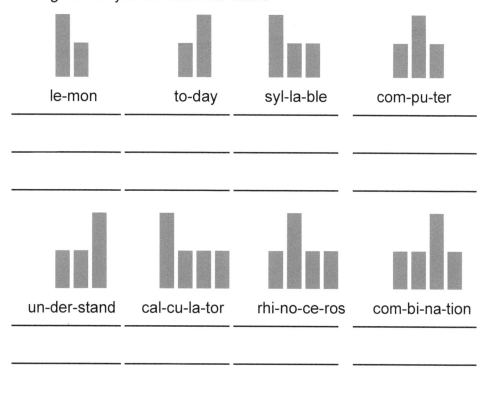

le-mon   to-day   syl-la-ble   com-pu-ter

_____   _____   _____   _____

_____   _____   _____   _____

_____   _____   _____   _____

un-der-stand   cal-cu-la-tor   rhi-no-ce-ros   com-bi-na-tion

_____   _____   _____   _____

_____   _____   _____   _____

_____   _____   _____   _____

Note: These eight patterns are the most common in English. We have deliberately decided not to include the least common patterns, that is, words with more than four syllables.

ACTIVITY D5. NUMBER OF SYLLABLES

Group the following words according to the number of syllables they have.

before	surprise	have	responsible
massage	adolescent	likes	family
comfortable	microphone	beautiful	eye

Example: Word with two syllables   bookcase

Words with:

one syllable

_____   _____   _____

two syllables

_____   _____   _____

three syllables

_____   _____   _____

four syllables

_____   _____   _____

E. STRESS WITHIN COMPLEX WORDS

In this section, we will focus on complex words and how stress is marked within them. We distinguish between two types of affix: inflectional and derivational. All inflectional affixes are suffixes, that is, they are added at the end of root words, such as plural forms and regular past tenses. Inflectional affixes only affect the grammatical structure of the word; they do not change the meaning of the root word, nor do they affect the position of the stress. Unlike inflectional affixes, derivational affixes can be added either at the beginning of root words as prefixes or at the end as suffixes. While all derivational affixes affect the meaning of a root word, not all of them will trigger the shift of stress.

In the section, we also discuss compound words. A compound word is a combination of two or more words that means one thing. The words in a compound word can occur independently elsewhere. There are three types of compound words: closed, open and hyphenated. Marking the stress within compound words can sometimes be a challenge. Generally, stress placement in closed compound words follows a similar pattern as in single words. Open compound words are treated as two separate single words. There is still a lot of debate around hyphenated compound words: should they be treated as separate or single words? While stress placement in the first two categories – closed and open compounds – follows existing patterns, the last category – hyphenated compounds – remains an issue for debate.

E1. WORDS WITH AFFIXES

Words such as *act, happy* and *slave* are known as content or lexical words. Content words can be nouns, verbs, adjectives or adverbs. Most content words can change their forms by having affixes added to their root forms. There are two types of affix: inflectional and derivational.

Inflectional affixes are all suffixes, that is, they are all added at the end of a root word. Inflectional affixes do not change the meaning of the root word they are attached to. They only affect the grammatical structure of the root word; they do not change the basic meaning of the word, nor do they change the stress pattern of the word. Here are some examples of inflectional affixes:

Table E.1. The inflectional affixes

Root word	Inflectional affix	New word
book	plural -**s**	book**s**
box	plural -**es**	box**es**
play	third person -**s**	he play**s**
wish	third person -**es**	she wish**es**
look	present participle -**ing**	look**ing**
tall	comparative -**er**	tall**er** (than)
long	superlative -**est**	(the) long**est**
cook	past tense -**ed**	cook**ed**
eat	past participle -**en**	eat**en**

Derivational affixes include prefixes and suffixes. Most derivational affixes are suffixes. Unlike inflectional suffixes, derivational suffixes change not only the part of speech of the root word they are attached to but also the meaning. Examples of derivational affixes are given in Tables E.5–E.8.

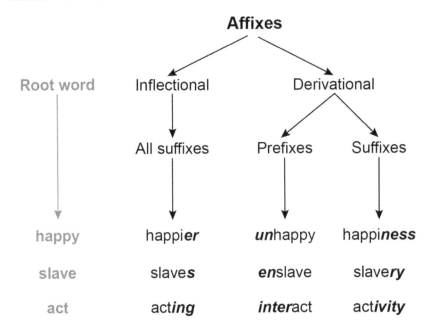

Figure E.1. The structure of word affixes

The three selected root words, *happy*, *slave* and *act*, perfectly illustrate the different types of affixes. The inflectional suffixes -er, -s and -ing do not change the part of speech of the root words. They simply add grammatical functions to the original words. However, the derivational prefixes un-, en- and inter- and the suffixes -ness, -ry and -ivity noticeably change the meanings of the words they are added to.

The new word *unhappy* means 'not happy'; *happiness* means 'the state of being happy'. Equally, the new word *enslave* means 'to make a slave of', while *slavery* means 'the state of being a slave'. The same principle applies to the verb *act*. The new word *interact* means 'act with each other' and *activity* stands for 'the quality or state of being active'.

As can be seen, the different parts added to the root words have different functions. In addition to adding one or more syllables, they can change:

a) The class of the root word: *slave* becomes *slaves*. The class of the word changes from singular to plural.
b) The meaning of the word: adding un- to *happy* changes it to *unhappy*, which is the opposite of being happy.
c) The position of stress: *'act* shifts to *ac'tivity*. The stress moves from *ac* in the original word to *ti* in the new word.

E2. STRESS PLACEMENT WITHIN WORDS WITH AFFIXES

Words with inflectional affixes

Inflectional affixes can either affect the grammatical class of a word or add an extra syllable. They can also affect the pronunciation of the added syllable, as illustrated here.

Regular past tense

One of those inflectional affixes that seems to affect pronunciation is the regular past tense. When marking the past tense of regular verbs, the suffix -ed may take different pronunciations. The following verbs all take -ed in the past but are pronounced differently, either as /t/, /d/ or /ɪd/:

Table E.2. The regular past tense <ed>

/d/	/t/	/ɪd/
agreed	asked	activated
believed	finished	added
called	helped	contacted
changed	jumped	indicated
enjoyed	laughed	needed
involved	pinched	regarded
listened	produced	rejected
lived	pushed	reminded
rescued	rushed	started
solved	sulked	waited

1) -ed is generally pronounced as /t/ in verbs ending with an unvoiced (voiceless) consonant such as /p/, /k/, /s/, /f/, /θ/ or /ʃ/, except /t/. The resulting word will have the same number of syllables as the root verb.

2) -ed is generally pronounced as /d/ in verbs ending with a vowel or a voiced consonant like /b/, /g/, /ʒ/, /m/, /n/, except /d/. Again, the resulting word will have the same number of syllables as the root verb.

3) When a verb ends in /t/ or /d/, -ed is pronounced /ɪd/, adding another syllable to it.

Regular versus irregular past tense

The way verbs form their past tense in English depends on whether they are regular or irregular. Whenever the past tense is formed by adding -ed at the end of the verbs, those verbs are described either as *regular, weak* or *inflectional* (see Palmer, 1987, and N. Mayala, 1991). However, when the past tense is formed in different ways, such as a change of a vowel or consonant in the basic unit, those verbs are described as *irregular, strong* or *lexical* verbs.

Different phonological tendencies seem to apply differently depending on the nature of the verbs. Let us illustrate two of those tendencies:

1) Most verbs ending in a lateral or an alveolar sound, such as *smell, spell, burn* and *learn*, will normally form their past tense with -ed, but a devoicing rule on the -ed suffix appears to cause a change in the sound production. This is the result of the phonological tendency:

Verb	Regular past	Devoiced past
burn	burned	burnt
learn	learned	learnt
smell	smelled	smelt
spell	spelled	spelt

Research shows that native speakers tend to favour the devoiced form, possibly because it is easier to articulate.

2) It is further argued (Palmer, 1987) that several verbs with a long vowel /i:/, such as *feel*, *keep*, *sleep*, *sweep*, *weep* and so on, have their long vowel shortened when the suffix -ed is added. So they become *felt, kept, slept, swept, wept* in the past tense. However, such vowel shortening does not seem to apply to many other verbs, like *knee – kneed*, or *peel – peeled*.

As is often the case with many concepts described in this book, one can only refer to general tendencies rather than to rules when analysing the principles behind certain phonological behaviours.

Plural inflectional suffixes

The inflectional suffixes -s and -es for plural forms tend to affect the pronunciation of the added syllable. The regular inflectional plural suffix -s changes its pronunciation depending on the sound at the end of the root: /s/ after a voiceless consonant, for example, *books – /bʊks/*, and /z/ after a vowel or voiced consonant, for example, *bin – /bɪnz/*, or *bananas – /bəˈnɑːnəz/*. The plural suffix -es adds another syllable, as can be seen in Table E.4. Nouns that form their plurals in a non-regular way may also have an additional syllable. Here are some examples of plural inflectional suffixes:

Suffix -s		Suffix -es		Other suffixes	
badge	badges	box	boxes	appendix	appendices
judge	judges	dish	dishes	child	children*
massage	massages	dress	dresses	half	halves
phase	phases	glass	glasses	ox	oxen
surprise	surprises	watch	watches	wife	wives

* Note the change of pronunciation of the vowel sound /aɪ/ in *child* to /ɪ/ in *children*.

Words with derivational affixes

Unlike inflectional affixes, derivational affixes always affect the meaning of the root word. The affix added – either a prefix or a suffix – to the root word also adds an additional syllable. As a general tendency, words with prefixes have their primary stress shifted to the added prefix. Tables E.5–E.8 illustrate some of the most common derivational affixes.

Table E.5. Derivational prefixes adding one syllable to the root word

Prefix	Meaning	New word
bi-	having two/occurring twice/ in two ways	**bi**cycle, biannual, bicultural, binoculars
de-	remove/reverse/off/from	**de**activate, decrease, decentralise, derail
dis-	not/opposite	**dis**connect, dislike, disrespect
il-, im-, in-, ir-	not/opposite of	**il**legal, impolite, inactive, irresponsible
mis-	bad/badly/wrong	**mis**behave, mispronounce, misspelling
pre-	before/earlier	**pre**dict, pre-dinner, prehistoric
re-	once more/again/refresh/ anew	**re**adjust, reassemble, recalculate, replace
tri-	three/three times	**tri**cycle, triangle, tripod, trisyllable
un-	not/the opposite of	**un**do, unacceptable, unhappy, unbelievable

Table E.6. Derivational prefixes adding two syllables to the root word

Prefix	Meaning	New word
anti-	against/opposed to	**anti**biotics, antisocial, anticlimax, anti-war
auto-	by oneself/spontaneous	**auto**didact, autonomy, autobiography, automobile
micro-	very small (one millionth)	**micro**biology, microfilm, microscope, microphone
hyper-	extreme/excessive	**hyper**active, hyperconscious, hyperinflation
inter-	between/among	**inter**act, interconnect, international, interdependent
over-	too much/excess	**over**cook, overconfident, overexcited

Table E.7. Derivational suffixes that do not affect the position of the stress

Suffix	Root word	New word
-able, -ible	'comfort	'comfortable
	en'joy	en'joyable
	con'vert	con'vertible
-ess	lion	'lioness
	god	'goddess
	prince	'princess
-ful	'beauty	'beautiful
	help	'helpful
	suc'cess	suc'cessful
-ion, -sion, -tion	con'fuse	con'fusion
	cor'rect	cor'rection
-ise	'author	'authorise
	'critic	'criticise
	'legal	'legalise
-ism	'capital	'capitalism
	'social	'socialism
	race	'racism
-ist	art	'artist
	'pharmacy	'pharmacist
	'piano	'pianist
-less	fear	'fearless
	home	'homeless
	'power	'powerless
-ly	calm	'calmly
	'careful	'carefully
	slow	'slowly
-ment	de'velop	de'velopment
	e'quip	e'quipment
	'settle	'settlement
-ness	'happy	'happiness
	kind	'kindness
	weak	'weakness
-ous, -ious	fame	'famous
	nerve	'nervous
	'fury	'furious
-ship	friend	'friendship
	'leader	'leadership
	'partner	'partnership

Table E.8. Derivational suffixes that shift the position of the stress

Suffix	Root word	New word
-ical, -al	ˈalphabet	ˌalphaˈbetical
	biˈology	ˌbioˈlogical
	geˈography	ˌgeoˈgraphical
	phiˈlosophy	ˌphiloˈsophical
-ion, -sion, -tion	deˈfine	ˌdefiˈnition
	ˈdifferent	ˌdifferenˈtiation
	ˈpermit	perˈmission
	preˈsent	ˌpresenˈtation
-ity, -ty	ˈactive	acˈtivity
	ˈflexible	ˌflexiˈbility
	ˈmature	maˈturity
	ˈpossible	ˌpossiˈbility
-eous	ˈcourage	couˈrageous

E3. Understanding compound words

Many English words are formed from two or more words that occur together. They are known as compound words. Overall, the term 'compound' can be understood as a combination of two or more words that may occur independently elsewhere. As for their meanings, it is generally agreed that the two or more words are linked together to mean one thing.

However, there is a lot of inconsistency in the way compound words are defined, spelt or stressed (Fudge, 1984). From a historical point of view, some compound words appear to have metamorphosed over time: starting as two words, they were later joined by a hyphen for a time before eventually becoming one word. There are three main categories of compounds:

Closed compound words: these are written together as a single word.

Open compound words: these are written as two separate words.

Hyphenated compound words: these are two words with a hyphen between them.

Here are a few common examples of compound words:

Table E.9. Types of compound words in different dictionaries

Cambridge dictionary	Chambers dictionary	Collins dictionary	Oxford dictionary
bookmark	bookmark	bookmark	bookmark
car ferry	car ferry	-	car ferry
childminder	childminder	childminder	childminder
cell phone	cellphone	cellphone	cell phone
helpdesk	helpdesk	-	help desk
goldfish	goldfish	goldfish	goldfish
on-site	on-site	-	on-site/onsite
well-being	wellbeing	wellbeing	well-being

As can be seen in Table E.9, the major dictionaries still disagree as to how compound words should be written. Furthermore, this book's scope is simply pronunciation and not morphology. The only aspect of compound words relevant to the present analysis is stress placement, not the historical reasons behind the way compound words were formed and their meanings. When attempting to spell a compound word, our advice is to use an authoritative dictionary, like those referred to in Table E.9.

E4. STRESS PLACEMENT WITHIN COMPOUND WORDS

Closed compound words are generally treated as single words and are likely to have their primary stress on the first syllable of the first word, as in *bookcase* or *blackboard*. With *open compounds*, the general tendency is to stress both words as two separate words. The tendency in stress placement for *hyphenated compounds* is not always clear.

As seen through the examples in Table E.9, there are serious challenges in recognising the actual concept of *compound*. Does it mean two words joined to create a new word? Does it mean two separate words that keep their individual meanings? Does a compound word function as a unit? There are no clear answers to all these questions.

Furthermore, it is not obvious that everyone can identify the relationship between the different elements of a compound. That is, how can we tell which elements of a compound carry the 'new/important' information in the set? Keeping in mind all these challenges, one cannot take it for granted that students will accurately guess where the stress is going to fall within a compound word.

ACTIVITY E1. INFLECTIONAL AFFIXES

Find five examples of different inflectional affixes that can be added to root words. What type of change does the inflectional affix add to the root word? An example has been given for you.

Root word	Inflectional affix	Change to the root word
short	-er	shorter (comparative form)
box		
long		
child		
book		
play		

ACTIVITY E2. DERIVATIONAL AFFIXES

Find root words to match with the derivational affixes. Which new words are created? An example has been given for you.

Root word	Derivational affix	New word
beauty	-ful	beautiful
	-ical	
	-eous	
	-tion/-ion	
	-ity	
	-ness	
	-ship	

ACTIVITY E3. DERIVATIONAL AFFIXES (PREFIXES AND SUFFIXES)

Find derivational prefixes and suffixes that can go with the root words listed on the left. What are the new words? An example has been given for you.

Root word	Prefix	Suffix	New word
friend	un-	-ly	unfriendly
active			
biography			
happy			
cook			
respect			

ACTIVITY E4. COMPOUND WORDS

Give three examples for each of these compound word types.

Closed compound words	Open compound words	Hyphenated compound words

F. ASPECTS OF CONNECTED SPEECH

Section F outlines English native speakers' natural ability to link sounds as well as combine words into longer units of speech. Sounds are combined to form words, and words can be combined to form short speech units, such as phrases and sentences. These combinations constitute the starting point of spoken language. When two or more words are spoken together, native speakers usually link the pronunciation of the sounds between words to produce smooth and continuous speech.

Some of the basic features of connected speech include contraction, elision, consonant sound linking, vowel sound linking, strong and weak syllables, tonic stress and contrastive stress.

Connected speech is also characterised by the distinction between stressed (strong) and unstressed (weak) syllables. The use of unstressed sounds makes English particularly difficult for students learning the language, mainly because the unstressed sounds, often realised as schwa, are less audible, and less distinct. In the sentence 'Pe*ter is* going *to the* shop *to* buy *some* eggs', all the underlined words are pronounced quickly and are therefore less audible to the listener. The other words, *Peter, going, shop, buy* and *eggs*, are pronounced louder and stronger than the underlined ones. The difference between these two groups of words, that is, content and grammatical words, is discussed in Section F3.

Native speakers' speech is also characterised by the inclusion of *tonic stress*. The word that carries the tonic stress in a sentence is the most important word for the speaker. In normal speech, native speakers usually emphasise words which are towards the end of the sentence. However, the speaker can decide to use *contrastive stress* by shifting the tonic stress to any other content word in the sentence. In other words, native speakers can shift the stress to the word they want to carry their main message. Students should, therefore, be encouraged to pay particular attention to the word or words the speaker is focusing on.

F1. Words and utterances

Students learning English will quickly realise that it is a non-phonetic language, that is, the spoken language is completely different from the written one. This is the reason why the first section of this book focuses on the production of the basic units of the English language, the sounds. These sounds, also known as *phonemes*, have been described in detail throughout this book. Sounds combine to form words. Words that have two or more syllables require stress to make their meanings clear. For a student learning English, these are necessary stages which ensure their knowledge and understanding of these basic concepts are strong enough to help them move to the main feature of the spoken language, known as connected speech. Since people do not speak using single sounds or single words, having some understanding of how words combine to form phrases or sentences is an important milestone towards the speaker's ability to be understood in spoken language.

To produce appropriate speech, words need to be combined into meaningful phrases or sentences together with several other features that help communicate meanings effectively. Some of those suprasegmental features introduced in Section B will be discussed further in this section.

We will start by revisiting the difference between the written and spoken forms of words. Then we discuss the difference between words spoken in isolation and when those same words are part of connected speech. In the following short conversation, two native speakers are meeting for the first time. First, consider the words as they are written, and then think how those words will be said together before you check the phonemic transcriptions that follow later:

A1: Good morning. I am Peter. What is your name?
A2: Good morning. I am Mary. How do you do?

How will two students new to English approach their first meeting? Apart from cultural differences, most students new to English listening to this short conversation should identify a few areas that will capture their attention. We have highlighted four of them.

Words–sound difference: in English, the spoken form does not fully reflect the written one. This is one of the major features of non-phonetic languages like English. There are more speech sounds than there are letters of the alphabet. Thus, many of the phonemic symbols used for speech do not sound or look like the letters used in spelling. A more detailed analysis of letters and sounds is offered in Section C.

The conversation between speakers A1 and A2 is written in the normal Roman alphabet. However, the spoken form of the words, given here, has little in common with the written language. Here is the word for word phonemic transcription of the conversation:

A1: /gʊd mɔːnɪŋ/ /aɪm piːtə/ /wɒt ɪz jɔː neɪm/

A2: /gʊd mɔːnɪŋ/ /aɪm mɛːri/ /haʊ dʊ jə duː/

It is important to note that these transcriptions of words in isolation do not reflect the way native speakers talk. When words are used together in phrases or sentences and spoken naturally, they produce what is known as connected speech. Connected speech is smooth talking, bringing together many of the suprasegmental features described in Section B. Thus, the conversation above might look like this:

A1: /gʊ mɔːnɪŋ/ /aɪm piːtə/ /wɒts jə neɪm/

A2: /gʊ mɔːnɪŋ/ /aɪm mɛːri/ /haʊdjəduː/

Sounds like *oo* in the word *good* when they are pronounced /ʊ/, the vowel letter <e> in *Peter* pronounced differently as /iː/ and /ə/ and particularly the phrase *how do you do* pronounced as /haʊdjəduː/ are typical examples of a non-phonetic language like English. These words–speech differences are likely to be challenging for most students learning English.

Prominence of certain words: for listeners, certain words will be heard far more clearly than others. Those words with strong stress are likely to be content words and the less audible ones are usually grammatical words. It is important for the listener to remember that prominent words – words with stress – are regarded as more important by the speaker.

The omission of some sounds: when speaking naturally, speakers of English do not say all the sounds in a sentence. In the conversation above, several sounds are not uttered. For instance, *Iam* is uttered as /aim/; the sound /d/ of *good morning* and the /ɪ/ of *what is* are not pronounced. They have been deliberately omitted.

Some sounds undergo changes: in spontaneous spoken English, some sounds can be affected by other sounds around them. In the conversation above, the question *How do you do?* has become /haʊdjəduː/. This feature of pronunciation is known as *assimilation*.

More about all these features can be found in the next section.

F2. THE IMPORTANCE OF CONNECTED SPEECH

Section F1, *Words and utterances*, is a good starting point for connected speech. It gives us some evidence in support of the view that English native speakers do not communicate using words in isolation. They usually combine words to form longer units of speech. Words in isolation sound different compared with when they are used together in a phrase or a sentence.

Native speakers naturally create links between words to make speech flow more smoothly. They also make some changes to the pronunciation of sounds occurring next to each other, allowing spoken words to link together. The process by which words influence each other when they are pronounced together is known as *connected speech*. In simple terms, *connected speech* means spontaneous speech as opposed to the pronunciation of individual words. Connected speech is the most important feature of spoken English.

In this book, we have made a deliberate decision to limit our study of connected speech to only those features that can improve speech intelligibility. For this reason, we will not discuss the theoretical aspect of intonation, but an activity will nevertheless be provided to illustrate the concept. The main purpose of this section is therefore to analyse the effect of sounds occurring together as well as the impact of stress in connected speech. Let us consider the phrase *a cup of tea* in a sentence:

> I would like a cup of tea, please.

1) Words pronounced individually:
   /aɪ wʊd laɪk æ kʌp əv tiː pliːz/
2) Connected speech:
   ||aɪd laɪk ə kʌpəv tiː pliːz||

When each word is pronounced individually (in 1), the listener will clearly hear four different vowel sounds: /æ kʌp əv tiː/. But when a native speaker says this phrase naturally (in 2), one will hardly hear *a* and *of* because they are not stressed in natural spoken English. One will probably hear two words: *cup* and *tea*. The listener will hear something like /əkʌpəvtiː/. The word *a* at the beginning becomes almost inaudible, and the third word, *of*, will be reduced to a schwa sound /ə/. In other words, pronouncing all these words *together* affects the way individual sounds are perceived by the listener compared with how the same words would be pronounced in isolation.

There are different features that make links possible in spoken English. These features include *contraction*, *elision* and *linking sounds*, but also the use in speech of *strong* and *weak forms*. Each of these features will be described in some detail in this section together with some basic illustrations.

Contraction

Contraction is the most common feature of connected speech in spoken English. It occurs when two words are pronounced together as one word. The use of personal pronouns with the verbs *be* and *have* and their negative forms represent the main areas where contraction occurs. The following examples illustrate some cases of contraction:

1) She is a teacher.	She's a teacher.
2) We would like to come.	We'd like to come.
3) He has got everything he wants.	He's got everything he wants.
4) They will not arrive on time.	They won't arrive on time.
5) Do not touch my face.	Don't touch my face.
6) Oh yeah, I have heard about it.	Oh yeah, I've heard about it.
7) They are not allowed to go in.	They aren't allowed to go in.
8) Jaden cannot swim.	Jaden can't swim.
9) That is true, she is an angel.	That's true, she's an angel.
10) The college does not admit teenagers.	The college doesn't admit teenagers.

Contraction is represented in spelling by an apostrophe. It is also important to note that, while contraction occurs in natural conversation, the speaker may decide not to use it if they want to emphasise specific words. In any of the examples above, the speaker may deliberately decide not to use contraction when they want to emphasise a point, as illustrated by these capital letters:

1) She IS a teacher

5) DO NOT touch my face

10) The college DOES NOT admit teenagers

Elision

Elision is the omission of a sound or syllable in rapid spoken language. It is worth noting that elision only occurs in unstressed syllables. Also the elided sounds or syllables are present in the written words. The following examples show how elision occurs in spoken English:

Table F.1. The omission of sound/syllable in spoken English

Written form	Spoken form
interesting	/ɪntrɪstɪŋ/
literary	/lɪtrəri/
national	/næʃənl/
preferable	/prefrəbl/
take him	/teɪkɪm/
tonight	/tnait/
should have done	/ʃʊdəvdʌn/
Wednesday	/wɛnzdi/

Sound linking

The main links between sounds are: consonant-to-vowel linking, consonant-to-consonant linking and vowel-to-vowel linking.

Consonant-to-vowel linking

When a word that ends in a consonant is followed by a word that begins with a vowel sound, the speaker's tendency will be to move the consonant sound forward and link it with the vowel. In the following examples, consonants are pronounced together with their adjoining vowels. The linking is underlined:

1) Lea<u>ve it</u>.
2) Divine is <u>an an</u>gel.
3) Let's ca<u>tch up</u> <u>with him</u>.
4) Colin <u>wants an apple</u>.
5) That's fine, we'<u>ve eaten</u>.
6) Please <u>turn off</u> your mobiles.
7) Michael <u>lost it</u> yesterday.
8) You look worried, <u>what's up</u>?
9) <u>Speak up</u>, I can't hear you.

10) What a pleasure to see you! Come in!

In Section C3, we discussed *Consonant letters and their sounds* and devoted a whole subsection to the consonant <r> and its pronunciation. We mentioned that the <r> consonant at the end of a word is typically not pronounced. However, in connected speech, when the <r> is in word-final position and is followed by a word starting with a vowel sound, the <r> *is* fully articulated, to smooth the transition between the two sounds. Those links are underlined in the following examples:

1) For example
2) Where is Louis?
3) It is for us to decide.
4) The city is far away.
5) It is a matter of opinion.
6) I'm busy, I'll see you later on.
7) You're better off staying indoors.
8) Jacob likes his new pair of shoes.
9) Dad has been a teacher for ages.
10) There were four or five people in the room.

Consonant-to-consonant linking

There are two types of consonant-to-consonant linking: (a) when a word ends in a consonant and is followed by a word beginning with a consonant that is produced in the same place in the mouth, and (b) when a word ends in a consonant and is followed by a word beginning with a different consonant.

Linking two identical or similar consonants: when this kind of linking takes place, the sounds are pronounced as one, creating a bridge between the words. In the case of stop sounds, the stop part of the sound is held for a short period of time before being released. This linking is known as *gemination* or *doubling*, illustrated here:

1) Have a good day.
2) Linda and Jason had the best time ever!
3) Gift accepted with thanks.
4) So far we are having a nice summer.
5) Hélène and Paul were delighted. The place was so clean!
6) Have you seen Kingsley! He is a very big guy.
7) Sit down and pay attention – //Sid down//.

Linking different consonant sounds: when a word ends in a consonant and is followed by a word beginning with a different consonant, the two consonants tend to influence each other. The most common phenomenon is the merger of the consonants to form a completely new sound. The process is known as *assimilation*.

Assimilation occurs when sounds belonging to one word influence the sounds of other surrounding words. It must be noted that assimilation, just like the other types of linking, is likely to take place in rapid speech, not in words said in isolation.

Table F.2. Examples of assimilation

t + p	→	/p/	wet paint	/wɛpeɪnt/
t + k	→	/k/	hot coffee	/hɒkɒfi/
t + j	→	/ʧ/	don't you?	/dəʊnʧu/
d + g	→	/g/	bad girl	/bægɜːl/
d + b	→	/b/	loud bang	/laʊbæŋ/
d + j	→	/ʤ/	Could you?	/kʊʤu/

Some more examples to illustrate the outcome of assimilation of /t/ and /d/ with a following /j/ are:

1) You like her, <u>don't you</u>?
2) Pleased to <u>meet you</u>!
3) How <u>do you do</u>?
4) <u>Would you</u> like to see my daughter?
5) <u>Could you</u> close the window?
6) <u>Did you</u> want to drink something?

Vowel-to-vowel linking

When a word ends with a vowel and the next one also begins with a vowel, the link between the two vowels can produce a different sound. What generally happens is that a /w/ or /j/ sound is added between them. The process is known as *intrusion* because a new sound is added between:

1)	<u>Who is</u> your best friend?	/huwɪz/
2)	Gael prefers the <u>blue ink</u>.	/bluːwɪŋk/
3)	It happened right at <u>the end</u>.	/ðijɛnd/

4) How many do you want? <u>Do all</u> of them.   /duwɔ:l/

5) Christian phoned last night. <u>He asked</u> for you.   /hijɑ:skt/

Sometimes the linking sound is a /r/:

6) The policeman tries to keep <u>law and</u> order.   /lɔ:rənd/

7) The <u>idea is</u> a good one.   /aɪdiərɪz/

It is worth noting that similar links do occur in other languages, such as French. In these examples, where the links between consonant and vowel occur in spoken French, they are underlined:

a) Les <u>enfants sont allés en E</u>urope.
   (The children have gone to Europe.)

b) Je <u>suis o</u>bligé de quitter dans <u>une heure</u>.
   (I have got to leave in an hour.)

c) Je <u>les a</u>perçois de temp<u>s en</u> temps <u>en allant au</u> marché.
   (I see them from time to time on my way to the market.)

Such links, however, are not possible in phonetic languages (languages spoken as they are written) such as Lingala or Kikongo. The main reason is that all syllables (and words) in phonetic languages are pronounced with equal stress and there are no weak forms. Consider these examples:

a) Lingala: Bana bakende na poto (every syllable is pronounced: Ba-na ba-ke-nde na po-to).
   (The children have gone to Europe.)

b) Kikongo: Bana me kwendaka na mputu (every syllable is pronounced: Ba-na me kwe-nda-ka na mpu-tu).
   (The children have gone to Europe.)

F3. WEAK AND STRONG FORMS

The next important feature of connected speech is the difference between strong and weak forms. It has been argued throughout this book that when a word has two syllables or more, one syllable will be stressed and the other syllable(s) will remain unstressed. The stressed syllable will have the strong vowel (the strong form) while the unstressed syllable will generally have the weak vowel (the weak form).

In connected speech, such a difference is clearly demonstrated by the presence of content versus grammatical words. *Content words* or *lexical words* are the important words that carry the meanings in the sentence. They include *main verbs, nouns, adjectives* and *adverbs. Grammatical words* or *function words* are ones that make the sentence grammatically correct. They build the structure of the sentence and establish the relationships between the lexical words. They include *articles, auxiliary verbs, conjunctions, prepositions* and *pronouns*.

Content words usually carry the primary stress while grammatical words tend to be unstressed. Grammatical words are *less audible sounds* as they are *weak forms*. These weak forms (usually represented by a schwa sound) always occur in unstressed positions. However, it must be noted that content words with two syllables or more have both strong and weak syllables.

Let us illustrate the difference between strong and weak forms. The weak forms are underlined in the examples:

1) The advice is about support for students.
2) Pollution can be a major danger for health.
3) A jealous husband can only suffer in silence.
4) Peter is going to the shop to buy some eggs.
5) Her behaviour was not popular with teachers.

It is important for students to be able to distinguish between content words, grammatical words and weak forms. Content words tend to retain their strong form even in connected speech. Grammatical words tend to occur in unstressed syllables and hence they appear in weak forms in speech. However, grammatical words can be used in their strong forms in special circumstances when their role is specifically emphasised. In the following examples, the underlined grammatical words are used in their strong forms because they carry the speaker's main message.

A1: Who are you looking for?
A2: I want to talk to him.
B1: What are you looking at?
B2: I am sure this is for me.

Text box F.1 offers examples of grammatical words in their strong and weak forms:

Text box F.1. Weak and strong forms of grammatical words

Category	Word	Weak form	Strong form
Articles	a	/ə/	/æ/
	an	/ən/	/æn/
	the	/ðə/	/ði:/
Auxiliary verbs	am	/əm/	/æm/
	are	/ə/	/ɑ:/
	can	/kən/	/kæn/
	does	/dəz/	/dʌz/
	has	/əz, həz/	/hæz/
	must	/məst/	/mʌst/
	shall	/ʃəl/	/ʃæl/
	was	/wəz/	/wɒz/
	were	/wə/	/wɜ:/
	would	/wəd/	/wʊd/
Prepositions	at	/ət/	/æt/
	for	/fə/	/fɔ:/
	from	/frəm/	/frɒm/
	of	/əv/	/ɒv/
	to	/tə/	/tu:/
Pronouns	she	/ʃi/	/ʃi:/
	her	/ə, hə/	/hɜ:/
	he	/hi, i/	/hi:/
	him	/ɪm/	/hɪm/
	them	/ðəm/	/ðem/
	we	/wə/	/wi:/
	who	/hu/	/hu:/
	you	/ju/	/ju:/
Conjunctions	and	/ən, ənd/	/ænd/
	as	/əz/	/æz/
	because	/bɪkəz/	/bɪkɒz/
	but	/bət/	/bʌt/
	than	/ðən/	/ðæn/
	that	/ðət/	/ðæt/

F4. STRESS WITHIN A SENTENCE

Whenever English native speakers interact in spoken language, they emphasise those words that carry the meanings they want to convey. However, although most content words are stressed to some extent, the speaker generally decides which word will carry the *main stress*, that is, which word will be the most prominent in the sentence. There are two types of sentence stress: tonic and contrastive.

Tonic stress

The word that carries the tonic stress is the most important word for the speaker. In normal conversation, tonic stress is generally found on a content word either at the end or near the end of the *utterance*. Here are a few examples of simple sentences with the tonic stress highlighted in blue:

1) Joshua's favourite sport is swimming.
2) Junior lives in a flat in London.
3) The king will open the museum on Saturday.
4) Samuel and Jaden will be bigger in twenty years.
5) Louis is one of the funniest children I've ever met.

The concept of *tonic stress* must be understood as the speaker's intended meaning. What the speaker wants to focus on is given a prominent *pitch*. So those more important syllables or words are known as *tonic syllables/words*.

Contrastive stress

In normal speech, the key message generally appears towards the end of the sentence, as discussed under tonic stress above. In sentence 1) below, the expectation is that the speaker wants to draw the listener's attention to the time they will be leaving.

1) We will be leaving the house in the evening.

However, if the speaker wants to shift the emphasis to another content word in the sentence, for instance, house, they can stress the word house:

2) We will be leaving the HOUSE in the evening.

The new emphasis – HOUSE – contrasts with the normal expectation, as described in example 1). It is therefore important to note that a speaker may decide to emphasise different words in the same sentence to convey a different meaning. They can do so by *shifting the stress*. Speakers can also use *shifting stress* (or contrasting stress) if they disagree with what someone has said.

The shift of stress signals a change of emphasis by the speaker. In the following examples, all the content words can carry the contrastive stress to reflect the message the speaker wants to convey. The content word in capital letters carries the speaker's key message. The meaning of the sentence therefore changes with the shift of stress, as explained in brackets at the end of each sentence:

> DADDY always writes his letters on the computer.
> (Daddy not Mummy)

> Daddy ALWAYS writes his letters on the computer.
> (Not sometimes)

> Daddy always WRITES his letters on the computer.
> (Not reads)

> Daddy always writes his LETTERS on the computer.
> (Not stories)

> Daddy always writes his letters on the COMPUTER.
> (Not on the typewriter)

If the last sentence was spoken naturally, the sentence stress would fall on *computer*, as explained in example 1). However, the *shifting stress* in the speaker's intention brings new meanings to the sentence.

The examples further demonstrate that a stressed syllable is very much linked to content rather than grammatical words. While the stressed syllables, as in *DADdy, ALways, LETters* and *comPUter*, can be clearly heard, the other syllables, *dy, ways, ters* and *ter*, are unstressed, with some syllables being reduced to the /ə/ schwa, as in *ters* of *letters* and *ter* of *computer*.

Students need to practise using unstressed sounds correctly to avoid sounding *foreign*. The key message is that not all words are pronounced with the same force in a sentence. Native speakers are said to *swallow* some of the syllables, that is, they barely pronounce the unstressed syllables. Students' focus should be on reducing the tendency to pronounce nearly all the syllables with equal force.

SECTION F ACTIVITIES

Identify all the **content words** in the following three sentences. List ten of them.

I would like a cup of tea.

The police questioned all those who were involved.

Sheila is going to the shop to buy some eggs.

List of content
words   _____

_____

Put the following words into their appropriate categories.

who, is, the, in, has, and, from, he, but, does, an, at, them,
that

Articles   _____

Auxiliary verbs   _____

Prepositions   _____

Pronouns   _____

Conjunctions   _____

ACTIVITY F2. WEAK AND STRONG FORMS OF GRAMMATICAL WORDS

Here are ten commonly used grammatical words in English. Complete their missing forms.

Word	Weak form	Strong form
the	/ðə/	_____
has	_____	/hæz/
are	/ə/	_____
can	_____	/kæn/
does	/dəz/	_____
for	_____	/fɔː/
of	_____	/ɒv/
to	/tə/	_____
he	/i/	_____
that	_____	/ðæt/

ACTIVITY F3. STRONG AND WEAK FORMS OF GRAMMATICAL WORDS

In each dialogue pair, underline the strong and weak forms of the grammatical words. Write either **S** for the strong form or **W** for the weak form, as illustrated in the following example:

Where <u>has</u> he put the money?	**S**
He <u>hasn't</u> said anything.	**W**
A1: Where is she from?	_____
A2: She is from Scotland.	_____
B1: Have you done the homework?	_____
B2: No. Do I have to do it?	_____
C1: There is nothing here.	_____
C2: I saw it over there.	_____

ACTIVITY F4. LINKING WORDS

Say these sentences aloud and underline the words that English native speakers would naturally link together when uttering them:

I love it.

Bread and butter.

I would like a cup of tea.

The police talked to all of them.

Peter is going to buy some eggs.

G. EFFECTIVE COMMUNICATION IN ENGLISH

G1. WHY LEARN CORRECT PRONUNCIATION?

Let us introduce this section with a quote:

> Fred was prepared. He was excited about the
> innovative cost-cutting methods he had devised.
> His PowerPoint slides were exquisite, his
> handouts polished and his presentation of both
> was well rehearsed. But there was a problem:
> Fred had to deliver his speech in English, and
> English wasn't Fred's native tongue. Although
> Fred's expertise was clear, his pronunciation
> was not. He worried that if his words were
> not completely understood, his remarkable
> contribution would be undervalued.
>
> Cameron, 2012: XV

Fred is a talented and highly skilled senior manager. His written presentation looks perfect and his expertise is unquestionable, yet he is worried that his message might not get through because of his non-standard pronunciation.

But why should correct pronunciation matter? Are all speakers expected to speak RP (Received Pronunciation) English? Can we all sound the same when we speak in English?

While the answers to the last two questions are obviously 'no', the first question deserves more attention. If your speech cannot be understood – as Fred feared – then your message will be lost. When we communicate in spoken English, it is not necessary to sound exactly like native speakers, but what is important is how effective and intelligible our speech is. What matters is making sense of our speech. In the situation above, Fred's success depends on a good written presentation as well as clear and comprehensible spoken delivery. He will need correct pronunciation to be understood.

Fred's case shows that writing and speaking are two different components of language. Thus, while in many languages, like Lingala, Kikongo or Swahili, the words (the letters) are pronounced as they are written, in others, like English, there is not such a direct correspondence between written and spoken language. In other words, there is a direct correspondence between spelling (writing) and speech (speaking) in *phonetic languages* such as Lingala, Kikongo or Swahili, but there is no such letter–sound correspondence in *non-phonetic* languages like English.

Furthermore, English uses other features such as stress, linking sounds and intonation to effectively communicate meanings in spoken language. For instance, the difference between **present** (noun) and **present** (verb) is the result of a shift in the position of stress – shown here in bold letters. Thus, placing the stress in the wrong position in the word *present* will give the listener a completely different meaning from the one intended. Similarly, in natural and fluent speech, English natives do not pronounce words individually but say them together in a continuous stream. They do it in a way that non-native speakers may find difficult to imitate. English speakers – like all speakers – unconsciously use certain features that affect the production of English sounds. That is, English native speakers naturally use several features specific to the pronunciation of the English language. Fred's experience clearly shows that correct pronunciation matters.

In this section, we will focus on some of those key features that play an important role in helping improve comprehension in spoken English. Let us start with the most common sound in English, the schwa sound /ə/.

G2. Schwa sound /ə/

The schwa sound /ə/ was introduced in Section C3 when describing the consonant sound /r/ in final position. This is an important sound in English, one which is always used in unstressed syllables. The schwa sound /ə/ – as the most popular sound in English – can occur in several contexts, some of which will be described in this section.

In single-syllable words with weak vowel sounds

In many of these words, the schwa sound can be triggered by the consonant /r/ when it occurs after a vowel, as in the following words with diphthongs:

clear	/klɪə/
fear	/fɪə/
tear	/tɪə/
mere	/mɪə/
poor	/pʊə/
power	/paʊə/
tour	/tʊə/
dual	/djʊəl/
cure	/kjʊə/
sure	/ʃʊə/

In grammatical/function words in their weak forms

as	from	has	the	must
and	for	some	that	them

In their weak forms, grammatical/functional words are pronounced with the schwa sound /ə/ in connected speech. However, when the speaker wants to emphasise their message, the grammatical words may be pronounced in their strong forms (see description and more examples in F3). In the following examples, the grammatical word *from* is pronounced in its strong form in the first example, whereas it is used in its weak form in the second example:

> A: What country are you <u>from</u>?   /frɒm/   – strong form
> B: I am <u>from</u> the Congo.   /frəm/   – weak form

Both speakers (A and B) will be expected to say the same word with different emphasis, thus highlighting the distinction between the weak and strong forms of the word *from*.

In unstressed syllables

The schwa sound /ə/ is used in words with weak vowels or in unstressed syllables. In several English words, it is triggered in unstressed syllables by the presence of the /r/ sound. Students learn about the difference between stressed and unstressed syllables through noticing that stressed syllables have strong vowels in them, whereas unstressed syllables have weak vowels. In the following words, the unstressed syllables are underlined to highlight the presence of the /r/ sound.

Table G.1. The schwa sound /ə/ in unstressed syllables with the /r/ sound

Word with /r/ sound	Unstressed syllable
clever	/ˈklɛvə/
character	/ˈkærɪktə/
doctor	/ˈdɒktə/
grammar	/ˈgræmə/
nature	/ˈneɪtʃə/

(The symbol /ˈ/ is used just before the syllable with the stress.) In many other words, the schwa sound /ə/ occurs in unstressed syllables without the /r/ sound.

Table G.2. The schwa sound /ə/ in words without the /r/ sound

Word with /r/ sound	Unstressed syllable
about	/əˈbaʊt/
camel	/ˈkæməl/
connection	/kəˈnɛkʃən/
famous	/ˈfeɪməs/
falcon	/ˈfɒlkən/
lesson	/ˈlɛsən/
pilot	/ˈpaɪlət/
suppose	/səˈpəʊz/

An additional feature that students learn from the above examples is that the schwa sound /ə/ has different spelling representations. Those spelling representations help identify a wide range of word categories with the /ə/ sound in unstressed syllables.

G3. CONNECTED SPEECH: EXEMPLIFICATION

In Section F, we introduced some of the main features that contribute to linking sounds in connected speech. Making links in connected speech requires the speaker to have some understanding of a few key features used by English native speakers, such as contraction, elision and linking sounds. While native speakers use these processes unconsciously, students learning English may need to learn them.

Examples of connected speech provide students with samples of phrases and sentences as they will have been said by English native speakers. The first set of examples is based on short phrases and sentences. The second set offers examples of dialogues as they will happen in real-life situations.

Table G.3. Pronunciation of short phrases and sentences

Phrase/sentence	Words in isolation	Connected speech*
Bread and butter	/brɛd ænd bʌtə/	/brɛdn bʌtə/
Would you like tea or coffee?	/wʊd ju laɪk ti: ɔ: kɒfi/	/wədʒu laɪk tiə kɒfi/
Have a good day.	/hæv æ gʊd deɪ/	/həvə gʊdei/
It is up to you.	/ɪt ɪz ʌp tʊ ju:/	/ɪtsəp təjʊ/
The village is far away.	/ðə vɪlɪdʒ ɪz fa: əwei/	/ðə vɪlɪdʒɪz fɒrəwei/
What a great artist.	/wɒt æ greit a:tɪst/	/wɒtə greitətɪst/
Could I have some sugar, please?	/kʊd ai hæv sʌm ʃʊgə pli:z/	/kʊdai həv sm ʃʊgə pli:z/
It is so hot today.	/ɪt ɪz sɔ: hɒt tədei/	/ɪtsə hɒt tədei/
He ate all of them.	/hi eɪt ɔ:l əv ðem/	/i eɪt ɔlə ðem/
What are you looking for?	/wɒt a: ju lʊkɪŋ fɔ:/	/wɒt əju lʊkɪŋ fɔ:/

* The transcriptions of connected speech are purely for illustration. We do not claim they are completely accurate nor do we say that they are the only way natural speech sounds can be represented.

Longer conversations

In conversational English, speakers unconsciously link sounds and change them according to the contexts in which they are used. Here are two examples of conversational English: (a) Going on holiday, and (b) A picnic on the riverside.

A couple and their two children are going on holiday. They are at the travel agency. TA = travel agent; HF = head of the family.

> **TA**: Good morning. How can I help you, sir?
>
> **HF**: Good morning. We would like to go for a holiday in Zanzibar.
>
> **TA**: When would you like to go?
>
> **HF**: Possibly in November 2020.
>
> **TA**: Have you been to Zanzibar before?
>
> **HF**: No, not yet. We are going there for the first time.
>
> **TA**: Would you like me to book the hotel as well?
>
> **HF**: Yes, please. Could you recommend a few good ones?
>
> **TA**: Yes, of course. Spice Palace is one of the best hotels on the island.
>
> **HF**: Thank you so much for your help.

Let us see the same conversation in connected speech:

> **TA**: || gʊd ˈmɔːnɪŋ haʊ kənaɪ hɛlp jʊ ||
>
> **HF**: || gʊd ˈmɔːnɪŋ wɪd ˈlaɪk təgəʊ fərə hɒlɪdeɪ tə ˈzænzɪbaː ||
>
> **TA**: || wɛn wʊʤu laɪk tə gəʊ ||
>
> **HF**: || pɒsɪbli ɪn nəʊˈvɛmbə twɛnti twɛnti ||
>
> **TA**: || həvjə bɪn tə zænzɪbaː brˈfɔː ||
>
> **HF**: || nəʊ nɒt jɛt wɪə gəʊɪŋ ðɛə fəðə fɜːs taɪm ||
>
> **TA**: || wʊʤu laɪk miː tə bʊk ði: həʊˈtɛl əz wɛl ||
>
> **HF**: || jes pliːz kʊʤu rɛkəˈmɛnd ə fjuː gʊdwʌnz ||
>
> **TA**: || jes əv kɔːs spaɪs ˈpælɪs ɪz wʌnəv ðə bɛst həʊˈtɛlz ɒn ði: ˈaɪlənd ||
>
> **HF**: || θæŋkju səʊ mʌʧ fə jə hɛlp ||

Three days before …

Dad, Mum, James (a 12-year-old son) and Emma (a 10-year-old daughter) are planning a picnic.

> **Dad**: I am looking forward to our Sunday picnic. I can relax on my deckchair and enjoy the summer weather.
>
> **Mum**: That's a very good choice of activity. May I ask, who will oversee the barbecue?
>
> **James**: I will help. I will collect the firewood and set the fire.
>
> **Emma**: I will marinate the chicken, the meat and the sausages.
>
> **Dad**: There you are! We've got plenty of helping hands.
>
> **Mum**: Do you expect the children to take care of the barbecue as well?
>
> **Dad**: All right! I get the message. It isn't Sunday yet, is it?

On Sunday … picnic day.

Dad has come back from the petrol station. The car is ready.

> **Mum (talking to herself):** I think we've got everything. Oh, I'll take a bag of charcoal.
>
> **Dad:** Are we all ready? Have we got everything?
>
> **James:** Yes, Daddy. We've got the meat, the chicken and the sausages.
>
> **Emma:** The barbecue set is in the boot. Have we packed all the ingredients, Mum?
>
> **Mum:** Yes, my darling. Everything is in the car.
>
> **Dad:** Good! All on board. Let us go.

On the beautiful green lawn … on the riverside.

James and Emma jump out of the car. They run into the nearby bush in search of firewood; 20 minutes later, they reappear with a few wet twigs.

> **James:** This is all we found; there is no dry firewood anywhere.
>
> **Mum:** Do any of you remember it rained two days ago? Where would you find dry firewood?
>
> **Dad:** If I knew I would have bought some charcoal. What a disaster!

Emma: Please, Daddy, can we go and buy some in the small town we went past on our way here?

Mum: What if you can't find any in the small town?

Dad: Are you suggesting we should go back home? Well, I am not. I have my deckchair and I am staying. I am going to enjoy the sunshine!

Mum: The only thing Daddy packed was his deckchair. Come on, children! Get the bag of charcoal out of the boot. We are going to have a barbecue to remember.

This is the transcription of the conversation in connected speech:

Dad: || aim ˈlʊkɪŋ ˈfɔːwəd tə aʊə ˈsʌndi ˈpɪknɪk | ai kən rɪˈlæks ɒnmai dɛk ʧɛə ən ɪnˈʤɔɪ ðə ˈsʌmə ˈwɛðə ||

Mum: || ðætsə vɛri gʊd ʧɔɪsəv ækˈtɪvɪti | mei ai aːsk huː wɪl əʊvəˈsiː ðə baːbɪkjuː ||

James: ail hɛlp | ail kəˈlɛkt ðə ˈfaiəwʊdən sɛt ðə faiə ||

Emma: || ail mærɪˈneɪd ðə ʧɪkən | ðə miːt | ən ðə ˈsɒsɪʤɪz ||

Dad: || ðɛə ju aː | wɪəv gɒt plɛnti əv hɛlpɪŋ hændz ||

Mum: || də ju ɪkˈspɛkt ðə ʧɪldrən tə teɪk kɛərəv ðə baːbɪkjuː əz wɛl ||

Dad: || ɔːl raɪt | ai gɛt ðə ˈmɛsɪʤ | it ɪznt ˈsʌndɪ jɛt | ɪzɪt ||

On Sunday … picnic day.

Mum: || ai θɪŋk wiv gɒt ɛvrɪθɪŋ | əʊ ail teɪkə bægəv ʧaːkəʊl ||

Dad: || aːwi ɔːl rɛdi | həv wi gɒt ˈɛvrɪθɪŋ ||

James: || jes dædi | wiv gɒt ðə ʧɪkən | ðə miːt | ən ðə ˈsɒsɪʤɪz ||

Emma: || ðə baːbɪkjuː sɛtɪz ɪn ðə buːt | həv wi pækt ɔːl ði ɪngriːdiənts | məˈm ||

Mum: || jes, mai daːlɪŋ | ˈɛvrɪθɪŋ ɪzɪn ðə kaː ||

Dad: || gʊd | ɔːl ɒn bɔːd | lɛts gəʊ ||

On the beautiful green lawn … on the riverside

James: || ðɪs ɪz ɔːl wi faʊnd | ðɛəz nəʊ draɪ ˈfaiəwʊd eniˈwɛə ||

Mum: || də ɛnɪ əv ju rɪˈmɛmbə it reɪnd tu deɪz əgəʊ | wɛə wədju faɪnd draɪ ˈfaiəwʊd ||

Dad: || ɪv ai njuː ai wədəv bɔːt səm ʧaːkəʊl | wɒtə dɪˈzaːtə ||

Emma: || pliːz, dædi | kən wi gəʊ ən baɪ səm ɪnðə smɔːl taʊn wi wɛnt pɑːst ɒnaʊə weɪ hɪə ||

Mum: || wɒtiv ju kɑːnt faɪnd ɛnɪ ɪnðə smɔːl taʊn ||

Dad: || ɑː ju səˈʤɛstɪŋ wi ʃʊd gəʊ bæk həʊm | wɛl aɪm nɒt | aɪ həv maɪ dɛkʧɛə ən aɪm steɪɪŋ | aɪm gəʊɪŋ tə ɪnˈʤɔɪ ðə sʌnʃaɪn ||

Mum: || ðə ɒnli θɪŋ dædi pækt wəz hɪz dɛkʧɛə | kʌmɒn ʧɪldrən | gɛt ðə bægəv ʧɑːkəʊl aʊtəv ðə buːt | wɪə gəʊɪŋ tə həvə bɑːbɪkjuː tə rɪˈmɛmbə ||

G4. STUDENTS' LANGUAGE BACKGROUNDS

Learning to speak a new language is generally a matter of personal decision. While grammar is learnt to improve, for example, quality of writing, it appears that learning pronunciation usually requires a stronger motivation and purpose, such as achieving good grades in a language/linguistics department or becoming a lecturer in English in a higher education institution. Whatever the reason for learning English pronunciation, choosing the right resources and the right language pronunciation model can play an important role in achieving success.

As a resource for learning pronunciation, this book is based on one type of pronunciation model: General British (GB) English, also known as Received Pronunciation (RP). There are, however, across the world several different types of pronunciation model. The main ones are General American English, Australian English and Caribbean English, but there are many more.

When learning or teaching English, there is always a need to make a choice of pronunciation model to set as a target. One of the major problems our students face working within one pronunciation model (GB) is that many of them may never achieve the native speakers' standard, simply because they may never have the opportunity to meet or live with native speakers. Students may get near the target model, or they may simply develop an amalgam English. While many may worry about not achieving the native speakers' standard, the focus of learning must be to improve the type of pronunciation model that will allow them to communicate intelligibly with other speakers of English. Achieving intelligibility in communication should be considered, in many ways, as a reasonable goal for most students.

There are many other reasons why getting to grips with English pronunciation can be challenging for students learning English. The first one is the influence of the student's mother tongue. In French, for instance, speakers always fully articulate the /r/ sound. There are therefore expectations that French speakers learning English will pronounce the /r/ sound with full voicing to reflect the role of the sound in the French sound inventory, as this is a natural way for them to use the sound /r/, as in this example:

> Remettez les verres dans les armoires et fermez les portes

The second reason may be the fact that students might not have some specific sounds in their mother tongue. For example, for those students who do not have the schwa sound /ə/ in their sound system, the influence of /r/ that triggers this sound will therefore be completely new to them. These students – for example, speakers of Bantu languages – will need to adjust the musculature in their mouths to be able to correctly articulate the sound /ə/.

A third reason is that many students may hear the new sound through their native sound system. Their tendency will be to replace the target language sounds with their own. A lot of practice will be required to tune into the correct English sound system. This practice may include reading the /r/ sound side by side with the approximant /l/.

Table G.4. Practising the /r/ sound with the approximant /l/

/r/ and /l/ in initial position		/r/ and /l/ in medial/final position	
/r/	/l/	/r/	/l/
red	led	cord	cold
road	load	fire	file
row	low	poor	pool
rock	lock	rear	real
root	loot	steer	steal

Although most phonetic languages, such as Lingala or Kikongo, have several consonant and vowel sounds in common with English, the actual sounds are independent to each language. Similarly, the absence of weak forms makes it particularly challenging to speakers of phonetic languages to adjust to features such as the use of stress and intonation in English.

More challenging still is the fact that several English sounds are not found in most phonetic languages; sounds such as the vowels /ʌ/, /ə/, /ɒ/ and /ɑ:/ and the consonants /θ/ and /ð/ do not exist in the Lingala and Kikongo sound systems. In their early stages of learning, students are likely to use those sounds which are nearer to their mother tongue, like /t/, /d/ or /v/. For this group of students, Section A in this book is a must-read starting point. Learning to correctly produce individual sounds will give them the necessary confidence to move to other levels of learning English pronunciation.

APPENDIX 1. CHART OF ENGLISH PHONEMIC SYMBOLS: VOWELS

/iː/ be, key, see	/ɪ/ hit, lip, himself,	/ɛ/ assess, bet, desk,	/æ/ apple, bag, sand
/ɜː/ girl, first, circle	/ʌ/ but, drum, culture	/ə/ about, bitter, calculator	/uː/ crew, food, fruit
/ʊ/ book, could, full	/ɔː/ call, baseball, hallway	/ɒ/ motto, upon, salt	/ɑː/ car, father, garden
/eɪ/ break, face, day	/ɔɪ/ boy, coin, voice	/aɪ/ height, five, my	/ʊə/ cure, poor, tour
/eə/ care, chair, their	/əʊ/ boat, know, old	/aʊ/ down, house, now	/ɪə/ beer, fierce, near

APPENDIX 2. CHART OF ENGLISH PHONEMIC SYMBOLS: CONSONANTS

/b/ bank, number, tub	/d/ day, lady, head	/f/ fall, often, cliff	/h/ hot, behind
/g/ girl, giggle, egg	/k/ cat, cucumber, lack, kite, turkey, kick	/l/ lost, willing, tall	/j/ yes, beyond, new
/m/ moon, memory, team	/n/ note, renew, ten	/p/ pot, paper, cup	/r/ rain, forest, far away (with vowel)
/s/ say, passport, bless	/t/ teach, hotel, boat	/v/ vein, review, give	/w/ water, subway, wow
/z/ zinc, present, was	/ʃ/ shell, bushman, dish	/θ/ thought, method, bath	/ð/ this, father, bathe
/ʒ/ genre, measure, beige	/tʃ/ cheese, achieve, clutch	/dʒ/ generous, algebra, courage	/ŋ/ ink, kingdom, morning

APPENDIX 3. SHORT/LONG VOWEL SOUNDS AND DIPHTHONGS

Type of vowel sound	Vowel sound	Examples
Short	/ɪ/	hit, kit, sit
	/e, ɛ/	bed, desk, let
	/æ/	bag, land, sand
	/ʌ/	cut, drum, luck
	/ə/	the, a, about
	/ʊ/	book, could, full
	/ɒ/	lock, mock, top
Long	/iː/	key, these, week
	/ɜː/	first, girl, learn
	/uː/	two, food, shoe
	/ɔː/	ball, call, tall
	/ɑː/	car, garden, park
Diphthong	/eɪ/	day, face, they
	/ɔɪ/	boy, noise, voice
	/aɪ/	five, kite, light
	/ʊə/	cure, poor, sure
	/eə/	care, chair, their
	/əʊ/	boat, know, old
	/aʊ/	cow, house, town
	/ɪə/	beer, here, near

APPENDIX 4. SILENT LETTERS: LETTERS NOT PRONOUNCED

Letter	Examples
b	climb, comb, debt, lamb, plumb, numb
c (sc)	scent, scientist, scissors, muscle
d	grandfather, sandwich, Wednesday
g	align, foreign, gnarl, gnome, sign
gh	bought, daughter, light, right, taught
h	chemist, choir, chaos, honest, honour, hour
k	kneel, knife, knock, know
e	drive, hope, site, write
l	calm, half, salmon, talk, walk, folk, could
n	autumn, column, condemn, hymn
p	cupboard, pneumonia, psychology
r	better, bird, car, four, lord
s	aisle, island, isle, viscount
t	castle, Christmas, listen, often, whistle; ballet, bouquet, depot, mortgage
w	answer, sword, two, who, whom, whose, write
u	guard, guess, guest, guide, guitar

APPENDIX 5. SELECTED COMMONLY USED WORDS

Animals

antelope	badger	bison	buffalo	camel
cat	cheetah	chimpanzee	cow	dog
donkey	elephant	fox	giraffe	goat
hippo	horse	jaguar	kangaroo	leopard
monkey	mouse	okapi	pig	rhinoceros
sheep	squirrel	tiger	zebra	

Birds

albatross	cock	crow	dove	duck
falcon	finch	flamingo	goose	hen
kingfisher	nightingale	ostrich	parrot	peacock
penguin	pheasant	pigeon	quail	seagull
sparrow	swan	turkey		

Classroom

blackboard	book	break	cafeteria	calculator
calendar	computer	correction	desk	detention
dictionary	divider	equipment	folder	glue
grade	handwriting	headmaster	inspector	laboratory
lesson	paper	pen	pencil	ruler
staffroom	stapler	student	study	teacher
term	test	trip	work	

Clothing items

anorak	bag	belt	blouse	cardigan
coat	dungarees	dress	earring	glove
handbag	handkerchief	hat	jacket	jeans
knickers	nightgown	overcoat	pyjamas	raincoat
shirt	shoe	shorts	tie	tracksuit
trousers	umbrella	underwear	uniform	waistcoat

Family members

ancestor	aunt	baby	boy	brother
child	daughter	father	girl	husband
mother	nephew	niece	parent	sister
son	teenager	uncle	wife	

Food and drink

beef	bread	butter	champagne	cheese
chicken	chocolate	coffee	croissant	dessert
dinner	egg	fish	hamburger	lemonade
margarine	marmalade	mayonnaise	meat	milk
omelette	pancake	pepperoni	rice	salami
sandwich	sausage	semolina	soup	spaghetti
tea	vegetable	water		

Fruit

apple	apricot	avocado	banana	blackcurrant
carambola	cashew	cherry	coconut	date
fig	grape	grapefruit	hazelnut	kiwi
lemon	mandarin	mango	mangosteen	melon
orange	papaya	peach	peanut	pear
pineapple	plum	prune	strawberry	

Furniture

armchair	bed	bureau	camcorder	chair
chandelier	chiffonier	computer	container	cot
cupboard	desk	lamp	loudspeaker	piano
rug	seat	shelf	sofa	stool
table	telephone	television	typewriter	wardrobe

Games and sports

aerobics	badminton	baseball	basketball	boxing
chess	cricket	darts	draughts	fishing
football	golf	gymnastics	marathon	netball
racing	rugby	sailing	skating	skiing
swimming	tennis	weightlifting	windsurfing	

Insects

ant	bee	beetle	bug	bumblebee
butterfly	caterpillar	cockroach	cricket	dragonfly
dronefly	flea	fly	grasshopper	honeybee
ladybird	louse	millipede	mite	mosquito
moth	slug	spider	termite	wasp

Kitchen

blender	bowl	casserole	coffeemaker	cooker
corkscrew	cup	dishwasher	freezer	fridge
fork	funnel	glass	grater	jug
kettle	knife	mandolin	microwave	mug
nutcracker	percolator	plate	refrigerator	saucepan
sieve	spatula	spoon	steamer	strainer
tablespoon	thermometer	toaster		

Shopping

bakery	banknote	bookshop	butcher	buying
change	cheque	confectioner	customer	escalator
fishmonger	goods	jeweller	manager	money
newspaper	pay	pound	purchase	purse
receipt	reduction	sale	saving	shop
shopkeeper	souvenir	supermarket	wallet	watchmaker

Tourism and air travel

airline	airport	airsickness	altitude	arrival
bag	belt	booking	cancellation	connection
crew	customs	departure	destination	escalator
fare	flight	helicopter	hotel	information
luggage	map	parachute	passenger	passport
pilot	plane	reservation	seat	security
speed	suitcase	terminal	ticket	trip

Vegetables

asparagus	aubergine	bean	broccoli	cabbage
carrot	cassava	cauliflower	celery	chilli
chive	corn	courgette	cress	cucumber
dandelion	gourd	horseradish	huckleberry	leek
mushroom	okra			

BIBLIOGRAPHY

Ashby, P. (2005) *Speech Sounds*, 2nd edn. London: Routledge.

Ashby, P. (2011) *Understanding Phonetics*. Abingdon: Routledge.

Baker, A. (2006) *Ship or Sheep: An Intermediate Pronunciation Course*. Cambridge: Cambridge University Press.

Bauer, L. (1983) *English Word Formation*. Cambridge: Cambridge University Press.

BBC Learning English (2015) *Pronunciation Tips*, bbc.co.uk.

British Council (2011) *English for Teaching 1*, Course book, www.teachingenglish. org.uk.

British Council (2011) *English for Teaching 1*, Trainer book, www.teachingenglish. org.uk.

Brosnahan, L.F. and Malmberg, B. (1970) *Introduction to Phonetics*. Cambridge: W. Heffer & Sons.

Brown, A. (2014) *Pronunciation and Phonetics: A Practical Guide for English Language Teachers*. Abingdon: Routledge.

Cameron, S. (2012) *Perfecting Your English Pronunciation*. New York: McGraw Hill.

Carley, P., Mees, I.M. and Collins, B. (2018) *English Phonetics and Pronunciation Practice*. Abingdon: Routledge.

Catford, J.C. (1988) *A Practical Introduction to Phonetics*. Oxford: Oxford University Press.

Celce-Murcia M., Brinton, D. and Goodwin, J. (1996) *Teaching Pronunciation*. Cambridge: Cambridge University Press.

Clark, J., Yallop, C. and Fletcher, J. (2007) *An Introduction to Phonetics and Phonology*, 3rd edn. Oxford: Blackwell.

Collins, B. and Mees, I. (2008) *Practical Phonetics and Phonology*, 3rd edn. Abingdon: Routledge.

Cruttenden, A. (2014) *Gimson's Pronunciation of English*, 8th edn. Abingdon: Routledge.

Crystal, D. (2003) *English as a Global Language*, 2nd edn. Cambridge: Cambridge University Press.

Daniel, J., Roach, P., Hartman, J. and Setter, J. (eds) (2006) *Cambridge English Pronouncing Dictionary*. Cambridge: Cambridge University Press.

DiCanio, C.T. (2010) *Introduction to Phonetics: Place and Manner of Articulation*. Lyon: Université Lumière.

Forel, C.A. and Puskas, G. (2005) *Phonetics and Phonology: Reader for First Year English Linguistics, Lecture notes*.

Fraser, H. (2001) *Teaching Pronunciation: A Handbook for Teachers and Trainers.* Sydney: TAFE-NSW.

Fudge, E. (1984) *English Word Stress.* London: Allen & Unwin.

Fromkin, V. and Rodman, R. (1988) *An Introduction to Language*, 4th edn. New York: Holt-Saunders.

Gimson, A.C. (1980) *An Introduction to the Pronunciation of English*, 3rd edn. London: Edward Arnold.

Hancock, M. (2013) *Pronunciation for Listeners: Making Sense of Connected Speech.* Liverpool: IATEFL.

HarperCollins (2006) *Collins Dictionary and Thesaurus.* Glasgow: HarperCollins Publishers.

HarperCollins (2009) *Complete French.* Glasgow: HarperCollins Publishers.

Hewings, M. (2004) *Pronunciation Practice Activities.* Cambridge: Cambridge University Press.

Hudson, J. (2018) *The Sound of English Pronunciation: A Practical Course in Standard Modern British (GB) English.* London: Anouka Ltd.

Hughes, A., Trudgill, P. and Watt, D. (2005) *English Accents and Dialects*, 3rd edn. London: Edward Arnold.

James, L. and Smith, O. (2018) *Get Rid of Your Accent for Beginners: The English Speech Training Manual.* London: BaTCS Global

Knowles, G. (1987) *Patterns of Spoken English: An Introduction to English Phonetics.* London: Longman.

Krashen, S. (1982) *Principles and Practice in Second Language Acquisition.* London: Pergamon.

Kreidler, C. (2004) *The Pronunciation of English*, 2nd edn. Oxford: Blackwell.

Ladefoged, P. (1982) *A Course in Phonetics*, 2nd edn. New York: Harcourt Brace Jovanovich.

Ladefoged, P. (2004) *Vowels and Consonants*, 2nd edn. Oxford: Blackwell.

Ladefoged, P. (2006) *A Course in Phonetics*, 5th edn. Boston: Thomson.

Laver, J. (1994) *Principles of Phonetics.* Cambridge: Cambridge University Press.

Marks, J. (2007) *English Pronunciation in Use: Elementary.* Cambridge: Cambridge University Press.

Mayala, N.J. (1991) *L2 Students' Knowledge of Verb Form–Function Relationships at Different Stages in the Acquisition of English as a Second Language: A Study of College Students' Interlanguage in Zaire.* PhD Thesis. Durham: Durham University.

Mayala, N.J. (1995) 'Integration or Differentiation? The Case of Bilingual Students', in Hart, S. (ed), *Differentiation and the Secondary Curriculum: Debates and Dilemmas.* London: Routledge.

Mayala, N.J. (2007) *Guidelines and Policies: A Handbook for Teachers Working with Bilingual Students* (unpublished). Barking and Dagenham.

Meyer, C. (2009) *Introducing English Linguistics.* Cambridge: Cambridge University Press.

Mongaba, S. (2019) *Dictionnaire Français – English – Lingala – Kikongo – Kiswahili – Tshiluba*. Bruxelles: Editions Mabiki.

O'Connor, J.D. (2013) *Better English Pronunciation*, 2nd edn. Cambridge: Cambridge University Press.

Odden, D. (2005) *Introducing Phonology*. Cambridge: Cambridge University Press.

Palmer, F.R. (1987) *The English Verb*. London: Longman.

Radford, J. et al. (1999) *Linguistics: An Introduction*. Cambridge: Cambridge University Press.

Richard, J.C., Platt, J. and Platt, H. (1992) *Dictionary of Language Teaching and Applied Linguistics*. London: Longman.

Roach, P. (2001) *Phonetics*. Cambridge: Cambridge University Press.

Roach, P. (2017) *English Phonetics and Phonology: A Practical Course*, 4th edn. Cambridge: Cambridge University Press.

Roca, I. and Johnson, W. (1999) *A Course in Phonology*. Oxford: Blackwell.

Scriven, R. (ed) (2009) *Collins Easy Learning: Complete French*. Glasgow: HarperCollins.

Shockey, L. (2003) *Sound Patterns of Spoken English*. Oxford: Blackwell.

Tench, P. (2011) *Transcribing the Sounds of English*. Cambridge: Cambridge University Press.

Underhill, A. (2005) *Sound Foundations: Learning and Teaching Pronunciation*. Oxford: Macmillan Education.

Upton, C., Kretschmar, W. and Konopka, R. (eds) (2001) *Oxford Dictionary of Pronunciation*. Oxford: Oxford University Press.

Viney, P. and Curtin, J. (1994) 'Survival English', in *English Language Teaching*. Oxford: Heinemann.

Watkins, P. (2005) *Learning to Teach English: A Practical Introduction for New Teachers*. Surrey: Delta Publishing.

Wells, J.C. (2006) *English Intonation: An Introduction*. Cambridge: Cambridge University Press.

Wells, J.C. (2008) *Longman Pronunciation Dictionary*, 3rd edn. London: Longman.

ANSWERS TO SECTION A ACTIVITIES

ACTIVITY A1. HUMAN ORGANS OF SPEECH

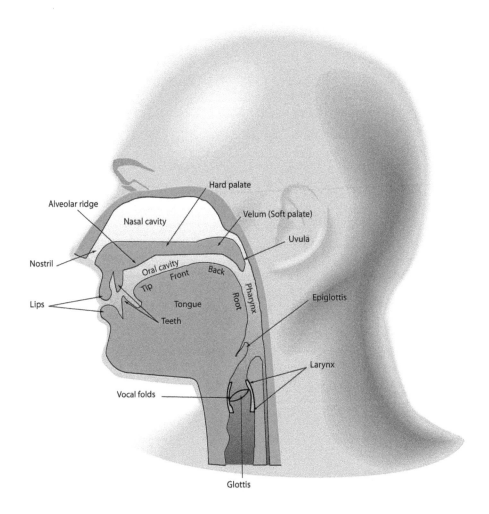

ACTIVITY A2. DESCRIBING SPEECH SOUNDS

What are these sounds called?

/b/, /p/, /d/, /t/, /g/, /k/   These are consonant stop sounds.

Describe how these pairs of sounds are articulated.

/b/ and /p/	These are called bilabial stops. They are produced by bringing both lips (labia) together, blocking the airstream from the lungs before releasing it as a small explosion.
/d/ and /t/	These are called alveolar stops. They are produced by bringing the tip of the tongue to the alveolar ridge to block the air from the lungs.
/g/ and /k/	These are known as velar stops. The air from the lungs is blocked by bringing together the back of the tongue and the velum. The air is released with a small explosion.

ACTIVITY A3. MATCHING SOUNDS AND ARTICULATION

Match the sound with the way it is articulated.

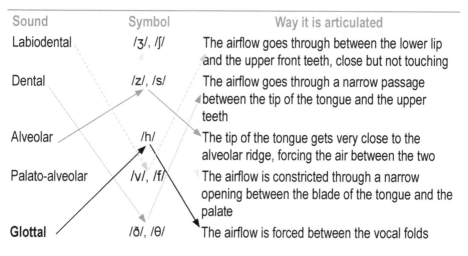

Sound	Symbol	Way it is articulated
Labiodental	/ʒ/, /ʃ/	The airflow goes through between the lower lip and the upper front teeth, close but not touching
Dental	/z/, /s/	The airflow goes through a narrow passage between the tip of the tongue and the upper teeth
Alveolar	/h/	The tip of the tongue gets very close to the alveolar ridge, forcing the air between the two
Palato-alveolar	/v/, /f/	The airflow is constricted through a narrow opening between the blade of the tongue and the palate
Glottal	/ð/, /θ/	The airflow is forced between the vocal folds

ACTIVITY A4. AFFRICATE SOUNDS

Decide which words start with the sound /ʤ/ and which ones start with the sound /ʧ/. Write them in the appropriate row.

sound /ʤ/   jealous   ginger   giant   job
_____ _____ _____ _____

sound /ʧ/   child   cheap   cheeky   choice
_____ _____ _____ _____

ACTIVITY A5. APPROXIMANT SOUNDS

Highlight all the words with approximant consonants in initial position.

paper	**lion**	shoes	door	**waiter**
mother	simple	**road**	**year**	girl
jam	**long**	**walk**	**lazy**	**razor**
yell	van	**red**	**yes**	**welcome**

Now put all the highlighted words in their appropriate groups – one example has been given.

i)   /l/   lion   lazy   long
_____ _____ _____ _____

ii)   /w/   waiter   welcome   walk
_____ _____ _____ _____

iii) /j/   year   yell   yes
_____ _____ _____ _____

iv)   /r/   razor   road   red
_____ _____ _____ _____

ACTIVITY A6. COMPLETE THE MISSING SOUNDS

This is a chart of the English consonants. The eight missing consonants are highlighted in blue.

Place of articulation

Manner of articulation		Bilabial	Labiodental	Dental	Alveolar	Palato-alveolar	Palatal	Velar	Glottal	Labio-velar
Stops (plosives)	Voiced	b			d			g		
	Voiceless	p			t			k		
Fricatives	Voiced		v	ð	z	ʒ				
	Voiceless		f	θ	s	ʃ			h	
Affricates	Voiced					dʒ				
	Voiceless					tʃ				
Nasals	Voiced	m			n			ŋ		
Approximants	Voiced				l	(palato-alveolar) r	j			w

ANSWERS TO SECTION B ACTIVITIES

ACTIVITY B1. SIMILAR SOUNDS BUT DIFFERENT SPELLINGS

What do you call words which sound the same but are spelt differently, such as *week* and *weak*?

Homophones

_____

Give three examples of such words:

site	sight
see	sea
there	their

ACTIVITY B2. SOUND VOICING

What do you call those sounds which are produced with vibration?

Voiced sounds

_____

List the words:

voice

zoo

genre

And what do we call the other sounds produced without vibration?

Unvoiced sounds

face

List the words:

safe

shop

ACTIVITY B3. REGULAR PAST TENSE WITH <ED>

The regular past tense <ed> forms used in the following sentences are pronounced differently. Practise reading aloud each sentence. Underline/highlight the regular verb and decide in which category you would include the verb.

1) The court rejected his not-guilty plea.
2) As a child, I **believed** the earth was flat.
3) My mum helped me finish my homework.
4) Jacob and Samuel **enjoyed** playing in the park.
5) Life in the village reminded me of my childhood.
6) The police officer **asked** to see her driving licence.

Now write down the verbs on the lines below, next to the correct endings – the first one has been done for you.

/ɪd/	rejected	reminded
/d/	believed	enjoyed
/t/	helped	asked

ACTIVITY B4. CONSONANT SOUND SEQUENCES

Here are five consonant sounds: /b/, /d/, /k/, /l/, /r/. Combine them in as many ways as possible to create meaningful new words, as illustrated in the example:

/b/ + /r/	as in	**brain**	**bread**
/b/ + /l/	as in	blank	block
/d/ + /r/	as in	drama	drive
/k/ + /l/	as in	clean	clock
/k/ + /r/	as in	cream	crown

ACTIVITY B5. SPECIAL SOUND COMBINATIONS

Some sound combinations can produce completely new sounds.
Give two examples of words with the new sounds:

| c + h | ⟶ | /ʧ/ | chair | cheese |

_____   _____

| p + h | ⟶ | /f/ | phoneme | photograph |

_____   _____

| t + h | ⟶ | /θ/ | thin | thousand |

_____   _____

| t + h | ⟶ | /ð/ | there | those |

_____   _____

| s + h | ⟶ | /ʃ/ | shine | shoe |

_____   _____

ANSWERS TO SECTION C ACTIVITIES

ACTIVITY C1. LETTERS AND SOUNDS

All these words have an <a> vowel letter in them. Highlight or underline the vowel <a> in the words.

about	baby	bank
dark	man	tall

Transcribe phonemically the words to reveal the differences. An example has been given for you:

bank	/bæŋk/	about	/əbaʊt/
baby	/beɪbi/	dark	/dɑːk/
man	/mæn/	tall	/tɔːl/

ACTIVITY C2. DIFFERENT VOWELS: SHORT, LONG OR DIPHTHONG

Decide whether the vowel in the word is short, long or a diphthong. List the words next to the correct description.

Short vowel	bed	hit	could	cut
Long vowel	car	ball	church	cold
Diphthong	care	face	kite	boy

ACTIVITY C3. SONORITY OF THE /r/ SOUND

Work out the sonority of the /r/ sound. Decide whether the sound /r/ is fully voiced, voiced or devoiced. Write the words under the correct column.

/r/ fully voiced	/r/ voiced	/r/ devoiced
rain	bright	strange
arrive	drink	contract
correct	frog	hundred
red	drain	spring
robot	dream	street

ACTIVITY C4. /r/ SOUND IN MEDIAL POSITION

When the /r/ sound is used in medial position and it is preceded by one of the vowels <i, e, o, u>, the presence of the /r/ may trigger the change of the vowel sound into an /ɜ:/ sound.

Now find three examples for each vowel with the /r/ sound in medial position.

<i>	shirt	bird	circle
<e>	serve	perk	herb
<o>	word	worse	work
<u>	burn	hurt	church

ACTIVITY C5. SCHWA SOUND /ə/ IN FINAL POSITION

Find three more examples for each word ending (-ar, -er, -ear, -or and -ure) with a schwa /ə/ sound.

calendar	grammar	popular	dollar
chapter	daughter	danger	hammer
clear	fear	dear	tear
doctor	major	motor	minor
nature	mixture	picture	pressure

ACTIVITY C6. SILENT LETTERS

Practise saying aloud the words in the left column. Is there any difference between the spoken and written words? Which letters are *not* pronounced?

Transcribe the words phonemically (in the middle column). Write down in the right column the letters which are not pronounced.

Word	Transcription	Silent letter
answer	/ɑːnsə/	w/r
climb	/klaɪm/	b
cupboard	/kʌbəd/	p
daughter	/dɔːtə/	gh
island	/aɪlənd/	s
Wednesday	/wenzdi/	d

ANSWERS TO SECTION D ACTIVITIES

ACTIVITY D1. CHANGING PHONEMIC TRANSCRIPTIONS INTO WORDS

Change these phonemic transcriptions into words.

/ˈænsestə/	ancestor
/ˈbæŋknəʊt/	banknote
/ˈbʌfələʊ/	buffalo
/ˈkɒkrəʊtʃ/	cockroach
/ˈmɑːdʒəriːn/	margarine
/ˈtiːneɪdʒə/	teenager
/pəˈdʒɑːməz/	pyjamas

ACTIVITY D2. STRESS PLACEMENT

Where is the stress placed within these three popular words? Mark the syllable with the stress on it.

controversy	/ˈkɒntrəvɜːsi/	/kənˈtrɒvəsi/
kilometre	/ˈkɪləmiːtə/	/kɪˈlɒmɪtə/
television	/ˈtɛlɪvɪʒən/	/tɛlɪˈvɪʒən/

ACTIVITY D3. PHONEMIC TRANSCRIPTION, SYLLABLES AND STRESS PLACEMENT

Transcribe phonemically these words; determine the number of syllables in each of them and mark the stress in the correct position within the word.

Word	Transcription	No. of syllables	Stress position
detention	/dɪˈtenʃən/	3	second syllable
avocado	ævəˈkɑːdəʊ/	4	third syllable
computer	/kəmˈpjuːtə/	3	second syllable
dictionary	/ˈdɪkʃənəri/	4	first syllable
lemonade	/lɛməˈneɪd/	3	third syllable
pineapple	/ˈpaɪnæpəl/	3	first syllable
supermarket	/ˈsuːpəmɑːkɪt/	4	first syllable

ACTIVITY D4. WORDS, SYLLABLES AND STRESS PLACEMENT

Find at least <u>two more words</u> to fill in each column.

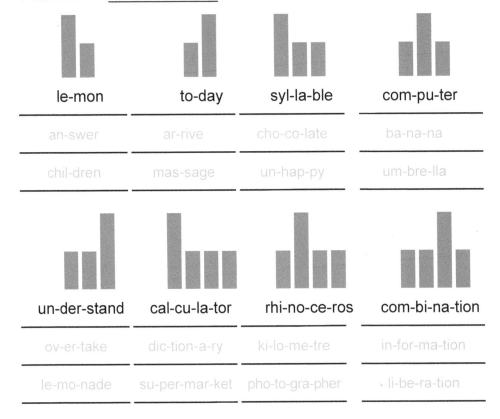

le-mon	to-day	syl-la-ble	com-pu-ter
an-swer	ar-rive	cho-co-late	ba-na-na
chil-dren	mas-sage	un-hap-py	um-bre-lla

un-der-stand	cal-cu-la-tor	rhi-no-ce-ros	com-bi-na-tion
ov-er-take	dic-tion-a-ry	ki-lo-me-tre	in-for-ma-tion
le-mo-nade	su-per-mar-ket	pho-to-gra-pher	ˌ li-be-ra-tion

Note: These eight patterns are the most common in English. We have deliberately not included the least common pattern of words with more than four syllables.

ACTIVITY D5. NUMBER OF SYLLABLES

Group the following words according to the number of syllables they have.

Words with:

one syllable	have	eye	likes
two syllables	before	massage	surprise
three syllables	beautiful	family	microphone
four syllables	adolescent	comfortable	responsible

ANSWERS TO SECTION E ACTIVITIES

Find five examples of different inflectional affixes that can be added to root words. What type of change does the inflectional affix add to the root word?

Root word	Inflectional affix	Change to the root word
short	-er	shorter (comparative form)
box	-es	boxes (plural)
long	-est	longest (superlative)
child	-ren	children (plural)
book	-ing	booking (present participle)
play	-ed	played (regular past tense)

ACTIVITY E2. DERIVATIONAL AFFIXES

Find root words to match with the derivational affixes. Which new words are created?

Root word	Derivational affix	New word
beauty	-ful	beautiful
biology	-ical	biological
courage	-eous	courageous
permi	-tion/-ion	permission
possible	-ity	possibility
happy	-ness	happiness
friend	-ship	friendship

ACTIVITY E3. DERIVATIONAL AFFIXES (PREFIXES AND SUFFIXES)

Find derivational prefixes and suffixes that can go with the root words listed on the left. What are the new words?

Root word	Prefix	Suffix	New word
friend	un-	-ly	unfriendly
active	inter-	-ity	interactivity
biography	auto-	-ical	autobiographical
happy	un-	-ness	unhappiness
cook	over-	-ing	overcooking
respect	dis-	-ful	disrespectful

ACTIVITY E4. COMPOUND WORDS

Give three examples for each of these compound word types.

Closed compound words	Open compound words	Hyphenated compound words
lockdown	car ferry	on-site
childminder	cell phone	part-time
goldfish	help desk	well-being

ANSWERS TO SECTION F ACTIVITIES

ACTIVITY F1. TYPES OF WORDS

Identify all the **content words** in the following three sentences. List ten of them.

> I would like a cup of tea.
> The police questioned all those who were involved.
> Sheila is going to the shop to buy some eggs.

List of content words	like, cup, tea, police, questioned,
	involved, Sheila, going, shop, buy, eggs

Put the following words into their appropriate categories.

> who, is, the, in, has, and, from, he, but, does, an, at, them, that

Articles	the, an
Auxiliary verbs	is, has, does
Prepositions	in, from, at
Pronouns	he, them, who
Conjunctions	and, but, that

ACTIVITY F2. WEAK AND STRONG FORMS OF GRAMMATICAL WORDS

Here are ten commonly used grammatical words in English. Complete their missing forms.

Word	Weak form	Strong form
the	/ðə/	/ðiː/
has	/əz, həz/	/hæz/
are	/ə/	/aː/
can	/kən/	/kæn/
does	/dəz/	/dʌz/
for	/fə/	/fɔː/
of	/əv/	/ɒv/
to	/tə/	/tuː/
he	/i/	/hiː/
that	/ðət/	/ðæt/

ACTIVITY F3. STRONG AND WEAK FORMS OF GRAMMATICAL WORDS

In each dialogue pair, underline the strong and weak forms of grammatical words. Write either **S** for the strong form or **W** for the weak form, as illustrated in the following example:

Where <u>has</u> he put the money?	S
He <u>hasn't</u> said anything.	W
A1: Where is <u>she</u> from?	S
A2: <u>She</u> is from Scotland.	W
B1: <u>Have</u> you done the homework?	S
B2: No. <u>Do</u> I have to do it?	W
C1: There <u>is</u> nothing here.	W
C2: I saw <u>it</u> over there.	S

ACTIVITY F4. LINKING WORDS

Say these sentences aloud and underline the words that English native speakers will naturally link together when uttering them.

I <u>love it</u>.

<u>Bread and</u> butter

I <u>would like a cup</u> of tea.

The police <u>talked to all of</u> them.

<u>Peter is</u> going to buy <u>some eggs</u>.

Milton Keynes UK
Ingram Content Group UK Ltd.
UKHW050440040324
438771UK00005B/88